AMERICAN BUSINESS ABROAD

Origins and Development
of the Multinational Corporation

This is a volume in the Arno Press collection

AMERICAN BUSINESS ABROAD

Origins and Development
of the Multinational Corporation

Advisory Editor
STUART BRUCHEY

Associate Editor
ELEANOR BRUCHEY

Editorial Board
RAYMOND VERNON
MIRA WILKINS

*See last pages of this volume for
a complete list of titles*

THE FOREIGN EXPANSION
OF AMERICAN FINANCE
AND ITS RELATIONSHIP
TO THE FOREIGN ECONOMIC POLICIES
OF THE UNITED STATES,
1907-1921

Paul Philip Abrahams

ARNO PRESS
A New York Times Company
1976

Editorial Supervision: SHEILA MEHLMAN

———◆———

First publication in book form 1976
by Arno Press Inc.

AMERICAN BUSINESS ABROAD: Origins and
Development of the Multinational Corporation
ISBN for complete set: 0-405-09261-X
See last pages of this volume for titles.

Manufactured in the United States of America

Publisher's Note: This work has been
reprinted from the best available copy.

———◆———

Library of Congress Cataloging in Publication Data
Abrahams, Paul Philip.
    The foreign expansion of American finance and its
relationship to the foreign economic policies of the
United States, 1907-1921.

    (American business abroad)
    Reprint of the author's thesis, University of
Wisconsin, 1967.
    Bibliography: p.
    1. Banks and banking, American. 2. United States--
Commerce. 3. United States--Foreign economic relations.
I. Title. II. Series.
HG2569.A55 1976   332.1'5   76-4762
    ISBN 0-405-09262-8

THE FOREIGN EXPANSION OF AMERICAN FINANCE

AND ITS RELATIONSHIP TO THE FOREIGN ECONOMIC POLICIES

OF THE UNITED STATES, 1907-1921

BY

PAUL PHILIP ABRAHAMS

A thesis submitted in partial fulfillment of the

requirements for the degree of

DOCTOR OF PHILOSOPHY

(History)

at the

UNIVERSITY OF WISCONSIN

1967

FOR

STUART GERRY BROWN

who encouraged me

TABLE OF CONTENTS

Chapter I

Founding American Independence
in International Finance

Foreign banks financed the great bulk of American
foreign trade during the 19th Century. Such long
established institutions as Baring Brothers & Company,
Ltd., Brown, Shipley & Company, and N. M. Rothschild
& Sons, with direct access to the London money market,
handled the heavy European trade. They granted credits
for imports, buying and selling sterling exchange for
remission to European creditors. Brown Brothers' branches
in Baltimore and Philadelphia, for example, financed the
imports of manufactured goods to northern ports against
the exports of Southern cotton to Liverpool. After the
Civil War, Brown's catered increasingly to the growing
raw materials needs of the New England manufacturers,
financing their imports of leather, wool, and Egyptian
cotton from British overseas connections. A half-dozen
such private banks, with their attendant brokers, dominated the American foreign exchange market, supplying
most incorporated banks and commercial houses.[1]

---

[1]John Crosby Brown, A Hundred Years of Merchant
Banking (New York: Privately Printed, 1909), p. 250-252.
The bank maintained agencies dealing in foreign exchange
in Charleston, Savannah, New Orleans, and Mobile.

American bankers' interest in developing foreign
trade finance increased in the 1880's in connection
with the growing exports of mid-western wheat. Canadian
banks with active foreign departments and close connections to the London money market moved into Chicago
and New York and won a substantial place in those
markets by providing foreign credit accommodations.
The American bankers, led by Lyman Gage's First National
Bank of Chicago, found it necessary in order to compete,
to establish extensive correspondent connections with
foreign banks that would issue credits drawn in foreign
currencies. The First National Bank of Chicago began
such operations in 1873 and by the mid-1880's it had
the largest foreign exchange division in the city.[2]
The Bank of New York became, in 1893, the first New
York bank to issue letters of credit against London
banks. Many others followed that lead: National City
Bank (1897); Bankers Trust Company (1903); Chase
National Bank (1905); Irving Trust (1913). The National
City Bank could boast in 1902 of foreign arrangements
"by means of which any sum of money may be paid out in
any city of the world within 24 hours."[3]

---

[2]F. Cyril James, The Growth of Chicago Banks,
Vol. 1 (New York: Harper & Bros., 1938), p. 495.

[3]Bankers' Magazine, Dec., 1905, p. 857. Wilbert
Ward, Bank Credits and Acceptances (The Ronald Press,

The growing volume of foreign trade was directly related to an increasing demand for efficient service in foreign exchange; but the development of the steamship and the transoceanic cable and the new banking facilities reduced the importance of the private bankers as suppliers of that exchange.[4] The formation of larger and larger industrial corporations with large export markets also increased the demand for better foreign banking facilities. As their export trade grew, manufacturers preferred to rely on their own foreign sales force rather than the services of the export commission houses which had pioneered American trade in South and central America and in the Far East. The export commission houses, small and undercapitalized by European standards, could not meet the growing internationalization of trade especially the pace set by the intensifying Anglo-German commercial rivalry after 1870. English

---

N. Y.: 1931), p. 9. The export of American manufactured goods doubled between 1892 and 1899. Alexander D. Noyes, Forty Years of American Finance, (New York: G. P. Putnam's Sons, 1898), p. 274. Memorandum in the Frank Vanderlip Collection, 9 Sept. 1912, Columbia University Special Collections Division. Vanderlip, who was vice-president of the National City Bank of New York, obtained a set of the government publication, Foreign Relations of the United States at this time, Vanderlip to Senator A. J. Hopkins, 8 Dec. 1903.

[4]For a description of the development of the mechanics of the American foreign exchange market, see Arthur H. Cole, "Evolution of the Foreign Exchange Market of the United States," Journal of Business and Economic History, May, 1929.

and German houses often engaged in indirect investment
in the firms that were their customers by extending
them credit for periods of a year or more. In contrast,
American houses rarely had enough capital, and usually
had immediately to discount their bills against foreign
customers at the nearest bank. As American factories
began to make direct sales abroad, manufacturers turned
away from the commission house methods of finance and
began to patronize banks that would accommodate their
needs.[5]

The nation's major discount market developed in
New York City where the heavy demand for foreign
exchange brought bills of exchange from every American
port. As the nation's largest port, and the seat of
American high finance, New York felt a constant demand
for foreign exchange to pay for imports, steamship
fares, interest and dividends on American securities
held abroad, and most important, for the repayment of
strategic short-term loans to European financiers.

---

[5]William C. Downs, "The Commission House in Latin
American Trade," Quarterly Journal of Economics, Novem-
ber, 1911, p. 121. B. Olney Hough, Elementary Lessons
in Exporting (New York: Johnson Export Publishing Com-
pany, 1909), p. 30. Also The American Exporter,
November 1910, supplement, p. 7. Archibald Wolfe,
Foreign Credits (Washington: G. P. O., 1913), p. 103
and speeches of Theodore Search, president of the
National Association of Manufacturers, Annual Report of
the NAM, 1897, p. 2; and to Southern Cotton Spinners
Association, 10 May 1900 in The American Exporter,
June, 1900, p. 13.

In either Chicago or New York, the average shipper (of
orders amounting to one or two thousand dollars) could
obtain exchange at rates comparable to those in European
markets.[6]

Foreign bills of exchange in francs, marks, florins,
and every other European currency carried American commerce. The sterling bill of exchange predominated,
however, because it was the basis of Britain's (and
many other nations') trade. As the demand for and supply of sterling was fairly constant its value fluctuated
within discreet limits. But American exporters who
billed their foreign customers in sterling immediately
assumed some exchange risk which disadvantaged them in
competition with British exporters. If the Americans,
in making out their prices in sterling, calculated at
too low a rate for the future conversion of sterling
into dollars, their prices tended to increase compared
to British prices. If they did not calculate at a

---

[6]It was the largest export houses and the corporations with the largest foreign interests, however,
which were interested most in the small differences
in foreign exchange rates and were aware of the
superiority of the large exchange markets abroad. The
American Exporter, November 1910 supplement, p. 7 and
B. Olney Hough, Practical Exporting, 3rd Edition
Revised (New York: Johnston Export Publishing Company, 1919), p. 44. The National Foreign Trade
Council called Practical Exporting, "The standard text
on foreign trade technique."

sufficiently low rate, they would get the business, but
lose money on the transaction through a loss in exchange.[7]

American importers also relied on sterling to
finance their trade. The importers' bank would arrange
a credit with a London correspondent that granted the
importer a letter of credit. On the strength of such
a credit, the exporter could discount his bill against
the importer with a local bank and receive immediate
payment for his goods. The local bank sent the bill
on to its London correspondent which presented it to
the London bank which first gave the credit. Twelve
days prior to the maturity of the bills (usually 90
day bills) the New York Bank presented the importer
with a bill stating the price of pound sterling credit
in dollars. In making payment in dollars, the importer
in effect purchased sterling to the amount of his credit
and a commission to the London bank for agreeing to
make the credit. The importer also took a risk in
exchange -- the variation in the dollar cost of buying
pounds.[8]

Behind the success of British exchange (and British
trade) were three important British banking institutions:

---

[7]J. Laurence Laughlin (ed.), Banking Reform (Chicago:
The National Citizens League, 1912), p. 99.

[8]Ibid., p. 98.

acceptance banks, foreign banks, and discount banks.
British banks had accepted (that is, guaranteed the
payment of) bills for foreign commerce throughout the
nineteenth century but the decade of the 1870's saw a
great expansion in this activity. With a ten per cent
increase in population and a significant increase in the
island's dependence on foreign trade for food and raw
materials a great increase in acceptances was produced.
These grew still more with a general increase in world
trade and the expansion of British banking which increased
foreign branches to more than 2000, each one devoted to
promoting the use of sterling.[9] Attracted by the great
utility of sterling, foreign banks began to move branches
to London which brought still more acceptance business to
that market. In 1914, all London banks generated the
equivalent of about $1,000,000,000 in acceptances.

At the same time, the importance of domestic paper
to the London discount market decreased sharply and
because of this the market became primarily an instrument of external finance. Nevertheless, it grew
steadily to keep pace with the demand for this kind of
credit. By 1891, three large limited liability companies and a score of smaller firms constituted the

---

[9]W. T. C. King, History of the London Discount
Market (London: George Rutledge & Sons, 1936),
pp. 265-282 passim.

London discount market. These grew in size until the war. In 1914, the three dominant discount corporations discounted £58,000,000 a year. By this time the working capital of the London market, which had formerly been almost entirely native, was more than half foreign.[10] During these years, several American banks involved in foreign trade, and developing their ties abroad, established branches in London. The Equitable Trust Company opened an office in 1895, and was followed in 1897 by the Guaranty Trust Company. The Farmers Loan and Trust Company was established in London in 1906, The Empire Trust Company in 1908. J. P. Morgan and Company organized a commercial operation called the International Banking Corporation with branches in the Far East to facilitate American trade expansion in that region in 1902; at the same time it established a branch in London to facilitate its extensive operations.[11]

By and large, however, the expensive correspondent system of financing American trade prevailed. Independent American foreign banking could not develop, despite the demand that appeared as early as 1890, without changes in the National Banking Act of 1862. That

---

[10]*Ibid.*, p. 282 .

[11]Ward, *Bank Credits and Acceptances,* p. 9. Also *New York Times*, 4 January 1903, p. 18.

act prohibited the powerful national banks from accepting commercial bills and from operating foreign branches.[12] Private banks and trust companies could and did make dollar acceptances but, with few exceptions, were not eager to do so when they could make adequate arrangements and tidy profits through their lines of credit with correspondent banks abroad.[13] Handicapped by the lack of foreign branches to supply the credit information on foreign buyers that was vital to the intelligent conduct of the acceptance business, and to make on-the-spot credit arrangements in dollars for foreign importers, the American acceptance business remained small. No significant domestic discount market developed around dollar exchange and, since it lacked the attraction for use in world commerce, foreign money markets did not compete for dollars.

These arrangements met the nation's foreign trade needs until the creation of the Federal Reserve System in 1914. But, beginning in 1900, influential businessmen and politicians increasingly felt that the future growth of American foreign trade required advantages that could come only from an independent foreign banking

---

[12]H. Parker Willis, "The Origin of the Acceptance Provisions of the Federal Reserve Act," *The Economic World*, 28 May 1921, p. 763.

[13]B. Olney Hough, *Practical Exporting*, p. 506.

system: branch banks located in the world's commercial cities; and a system of acceptance and discount banks at home. The American and foreign banks would also actively seek business for American clients. As middlemen between exporters and importers, the banks would encourage both American and foreign exporters to draw bills in dollars creating dollar exchange which the banks would sell to needy importers. In this way dollar exchange would replace sterling.

The acceptance of the bills by reputable banks would make them prime short-term investments in the discount market and attract capital to trade finance at low rates of interest. The arrangement would eliminate the risk in converting to sterling and the expense of commissions to British banks. Knowledgeable advocates of this policy predicted it would increase business for American banks, retain money for banking services which would otherwise flow to England, and increase America's international prestige.[14]

The Comptroller of the Currency recognized the desires of some of the larger national banks in New York and Chicago to expand their foreign operations by recommending, in his Annual Report of 1904, that

---

[14]Paul Warburg, "The Discount System in Europe," Federal Reserve System, Vol. II, p. 187.

national banks having a capital of $1,000,000 or more
be authorized to accept bills of exchange and establish
foreign branches. Domestic banking needs overshadowed
the demands for the reform of foreign banking, however.[15]
The disadvantages of dispersed reserves had exacerbated
financial disturbances in 1884 and 1893. The panic of
1907 underscored the defects of a system that required
special banking arrangements to borrow $500,000,000
from Europe in order to prevent the collapse of the
stock market and ultimately of the banks themselves.
The severe strain on European credit convinced influential bankers in America (and abroad) that the weight
of the American economy had become too great for Europe
to carry in emergencies, and that an American solution
to the basic problem could no longer be postponed.[16]

---

[15]New York Times, 18 December, 1904, p. 18.

[16]Noyes, op. cit., p. 327, quotes economist Paul
Leroy-Beaulier from the Economist Francais, 5 January
1907 as writing: "...there was a demand in America,
at any rate, for even more than its part of the world's
supply of capital, to be provided during 1907. But the
world has not got it; therefore, it cannot provide it."
The Bank of England had issued a warning to joint stock
institutions to stop their lending to the New York
market or face a 7% bank rate as the drain of gold from
England and Europe was becoming critical, Noyes,
op. cit., p. 355. By 1910, if not before, Paul M.
Warburg, a German-born expert on international finance,
could say, "...the financial machinery of Europe may
break down sometime under our huge weight." Frank
Vanderlip to P. M. Warburg, 1 March 1910, Vanderlip
Collection. For an international perspective on the
credit question see Arthur L. Bloomfield, "Short-term

Inevitably, plans for the implementation of a foreign banking system became enmeshed with the proposed reform of the system.

Nelson W. Aldrich, the leader of the Senate Republican majority, wanted to solve the basic problem of increasing bank reserves by allowing banks to use railroad and industrial bonds in place of government bonds as reserves, thereby ensuring a strong market for the paper of the newly formed trusts which had encountered great difficulty in placing their overcapitalized issues with the public. Most bankers, however, wanted a currency based on short-term self-liquidating commercial paper discounted at low rates by a reserve association.[17] More internationally-minded bankers saw in that kind of a system the possibility of discounting bills emanating from foreign transactions, and that could provide a base for an independent foreign banking

Capital Movements Under the Pre-1914 Gold Standard," Princeton University Studies in International Finance No. 11 (Princeton: 1963).

[17]This had been the recommendation of the Indianapolis Monetary Convention in 1898. See Taylor, op. cit. Paul Warburg was an early and forceful advocate of short term assets currency. See his Federal Reserve System, Volume 1 (New York: The Macmillan Company, 1930), p. 25. Vanderlip had endorsed Warburg's idea as early as 20 March 1907, Vanderlip to Edward M. McMahon (Fidelity Trust Company, Milwaukee). For James Stillman's point of view see Vanderlip to Senator S. B. Elkins, 20 January 1908, Vanderlip Papers.

system. Frank Vanderlip of the powerful National City
Bank of New York, and Paul M. Warburg, a German-born
international finance expert and partner in the important investment house of Kuhn, Loeb, & Company, were
influential spokesmen for that kind of reform. Aldrich,
according to his biographer, "veering toward a major
interest in foreign business, came around to this point
of view in 1908 when London bankers explained to him
the great value of a central banking and discount
system to foreign trade."[18]

While Senator Aldrich's Monetary Commission began
a detailed study of world banking systems in order to
tailor discount banking legislation to American conditions,
President William Howard Taft acknowledged these developing
techniques in banking services abroad and enlisted them
in support of national security interests in the Caribbean,
committing his administration to the so-called "dollar
diplomacy." Taft's program convinced a so-called "South
American group", which included the National City Bank,
Kuhn, Loeb, J. P. Morgan, and the First National Bank
of New York that a branch banking system in Latin
America warranted serious consideration.[19] While trade

---

[18]Nathaniel W. Stephenson, Nelson W. Aldrich (New
York: Scribners, 1930), p. 337-338. Warburg,
op. cit., p. 56.

[19]Vanderlip felt he had very close ties with Knox,

financing operations offered attractive long run profits,
the prospects of a lucrative business in marketing South
American government bonds aroused the deepest interests
of the four banks, all of which had influential connections in the American bond market.[20]   On the advice
of its field men, however, the group suspended plans

---

and their plan had the unanimous support of the Taft
cabinet. Vanderlip to Stillman, 1 May 1909, Vanderlip
Collection. Memorandum for Secretary MacVeagh, Relative
to Securing Legislation Authorizing National Banks of
a Certain Minimum Capital to Establish Branches in
Foreign Countries and to Make Acceptions, Milton Ailes
to Franklin MacVeagh, Secretary of the Treasury, 5 May
1910, Box 3, MacVeagh Papers, Library of Congress.
Samuel McRoberts (vice-president, National City Bank),
to Frank Vanderlip, 9 April 1910, Vanderlip Papers.

[20]J. P. Morgan & Company, Kuhn, Loeb, & Company,
National City Bank, and First National Bank to Philander
C. Knox, 12 July 1909, Numerical File No. 20606, RG59,
NARS. Vanderlip to Stillman, 7 May 1909, Vanderlip
Collection. Vanderlip observed to Stillman, 3 June
1909, that the Bank "...would permanently put us into
a most satisfactory relation with future government
financing in /South America7 and do it all with as
little investment ourselves as we choose to make."   On
11 June 1909, he wrote Stillman, "...the position we
will get in South American government finance will
probably compensate for whatever patience we may have
to show in the other direction."   To head the bank's
foreign operations they unsuccessfully sought the
wealthy Assistant Secretary of State, Robert Bacon, one
of the early directors of Morgan's Amalgamated Copper
Company. For the banks' connections to the bond market
see U. S. House of Representatives, 62nd Congress, 3rd
Session, The Money Trust Investigation (Washington:
G. F. O., 1913), Volume 2, p. 1669, and Volume 3, p. 129.
They thought the prospects were good enough to turn
down an offer from the large Anglo-South American
Bank for a share in the business if they abandoned
their own plan and worked through the British concern.
Vanderlip to Stillman, 29 October 1909, Vanderlip
Papers.

until such time as a depression deflated the then
existing boom in South America. A deflation would
cut the inflated values and permit cheap entree by the
American investors.[21]

In the meantime, Aldrich, in conference with
Vanderlip, Warburg, A. Piatt Andrew of the United
States Treasury, and Benjamin Strong, vice-president
of the Banker's Trust Company, worked out the main out-
lines of this bill and included means for foreign
expansion. The Aldrich Plan would have enlarged the
nation's credit capacity by allowing banks to discount
commercial paper in return for reserve association currency. To advance America's fortunes abroad, the bill
proposed to create a new class of commercial paper: the
90 day acceptance, guaranteed like the European acceptance by a bank or reputable merchant, discountable for
currency at member banks of the association, and saleable
in the open market. The acceptance could be made by
any reputable bank or merchant against foreign or domestic transactions, thus creating the broadest possible
discount market. Moreover, the association could
establish foreign agencies empowered to buy and sell
foreign exchange and so stabilize the foreign exchange

[21]Vanderlip to Stillman, 5 June 1914, Vanderlip
Papers. Milton Ailes to Vanderlip, 29 August 1910,
Vanderlip Papers.

rate and control the nation's gold flow. Foreign banking corporations, whose stock association members could
purchase, would actually finance American foreign
trade.[22]

But the idea of a central bank under the control
of bankers, which the planners thought necessary, caused
the defeat of this proposal. The triumphant opponents
did not for a minute object, however, to the foreign
expansion of the banking system. They even advocated
separate legislation permitting the foreign expansion
of American banking without delay, and supported the
idea of enacting that while the factions worked out a
new banking bill.[23] Instead of taking that alternative,
the Wilson administration included a branch bank and
acceptance system in its reform bill with the understanding that these were the recognized mechanisms of
foreign trade and necessary to American entry into the
field. The new plan, drafted under the direction of
Carter Glass, the Democratic chairman of the House Committee on Banking and Finance abandoned foreign banking

---

[22]Frank Vanderlip, From Farm Boy to Financier
(New York: D. Apellton Century Company, 1935), p. 213.
The National Monetary Commission Report, U. S. Senate,
62nd Congress, 2nd Session, Senate Doc. No. 243,
(Washington: G. P. O., 1912) contains the Monetary
Commission or Aldrich bill with an excellent explana-
tion. See especially pp. 27-32 for foreign aspects.

[23]Bankers' Magazine, October 1912, p. 343.

corporations in favor of foreign branches of existing banks. Not fully convinced of the safety of the new and untried bankers' acceptances he adopted them for domestic and foreign commerce, "cautiously to begin with."[24] Obedient to the Democratic platform, and over the bankers' objections, the Committee abandoned the central bank idea and established twelve Federal Reserve Banks. Warburg, in particular, warned that the twelve-bank system would produce unstable rates for commercial bills, adversely affect their negotiability, and discourage foreigners from investing their surplus funds in dollar acceptances.[25] But the bankers, unable to combat the prevailing distrust of privately controlled centralized banking power, ended their opposition and counted on the experiences of the system to bring forth the improvements they considered necessary. President Woodrow Wilson's appointments of men like Paul Warburg, W. P. G. Harding, and Benjamin Strong

---

[24]U. S. House of Representatives, 62nd Congress, 3rd Session, Hearings of the Subcommittee of the Committee on Banking and Currency, Volume 1, p. 633. Also see The Economic World, 28 May 1921, p. 763.

[25]Subcommittee Hearings, p. 81, shows Warburg's position on this. An excellent comparison of the two bills with Warburg's commentary may be found in his Federal Reserve System, Volume 1. Also see O. M. W. Sprague to Warburg, 19 December 1913, Warburg Papers, Yale University.

to important positions in the new system reassured the
bankers and modified their fears of government control.[26]

The voluminous hearings of the banking and currency
committee which produced the Federal Reserve bill do not
reveal a preoccupation with matters of foreign trade
finance. Yet there is little question that, as a later
Governor of the Federal Reserve System remarked, the
Act "was designed in large part to expand our trade with
foreign countries."[27] Geographical factors restricted
interest in foreign trade finance to the banks of the
major port cities and to banks which served the foreign
interests of the large exporting corporations. These
were primarily New York banks. Congress considered this
foreign interest distinct and necessary enough to
justify immediate support when it appeared that more
controversial matters would delay passage of a general
reform bill. The establishment of a stronger reserve

---

[26]Matthew Josephson, The President Makers, 1896-
1919 (New York: 1940), p. 487. Elihu Post called the
System "...an effort to transfer the function which that
firm /J. P. Morgan and Company/ has in a great measure
/been/ discharging..." Root to Committee on Admissions,
University Club, N. Y. C., 8 September 1913, Root Papers,
Box 106, Library of Congress.

[27]W. P. G. Harding, Commercial and Financial
Chronicle, 30 March 1918, p. 1290. For summaries of
discussion on the 6-11 see Paul Warburg, The Federal
Reserve System, Volume II and Benjamin Beckhart, Dis-
count Policy of the Federal Reserve System (New York:
Henry Holt and Company, 1924), p. 123.

position for the member banks of the new system helped
this growth by increasing the country's financial
strength at home and abroad. A rapid expansion of
American foreign finance followed the passage of the
Act, attesting to the support that it intentionally
gave the banks in this respect.

Chapter II

Building a Network of Foreign Branches

Despite lingering adverse feelings about the
Federal Reserve Act as signed by President Woodrow
Wilson on December 23, 1913, Frank Vanderlip felt that
his great bank, the National City, had more opportunity
than ever before to transform the entire country into
a field for its operations. "The difficulty," he
explained to James Stillman, "is in persuading a man
that an account with City is an advantage over an
account with another bank."[1] But he felt that foreign
trade services provided that advantage. Immediately
after the passage of the act, the National City Bank
sent a questionnaire to 5,000 manufacturers throughout
the nation seeking information as to which markets
needed banking facilities and asking suggestions for
the kind of facilities needed. Those interviewed almost
unanimously felt strongly about the need for credit and
trade information concerning South America. The interest

---

[1]Frank Vanderlip to James Stillman, 5 June 1914,
Vanderlip Collection, Columbia University. The National
Bank Act of 1863 did not allow national banks to establish branches. This forced the NCB to expand along
service lines. Encyclopedia of Banking and Finance,
6th ed., (Boston: The Bankers' Publishing Co., 1962),
p. 85.

was surprisingly general, Vanderlip wrote Stillman,
"and if I read the sings /sic/ at all right, it indicates that we are facing a very large development in
our South American trade relations."[2] But until the
Federal Reserve System completed its organization, late
in 1914 and the beginning of 1915, and provided the
discount market for bills of exchange arising from the
new trade, Vanderlip avoided positive action. "I do
not feel that we want to rush into this branch bank
business," he wrote his foreign exchange manager.[3]

The recession of 1913-1914 may have accelerated
Vanderlip's plans. The expansion of business activity
in Europe and the Balkan crisis caused an unusually
heavy demand for gold and the withdrawal of gold and
capital loan funds from the United States. The effect
was to weaken the credit resources of American business
and cause a contraction in the economy which lasted until 1915. For a good part of 1913, the physical volume
of business remained large because of heavy orders
originating from the boom of 1912, but after those orders
had been filled no current demand developed to bolster
business activity and the latter part of the year saw a
marked recession. The United States Steel Corporation,

[2]Ibid.

[3]Vanderlip to John Gardin, 1 March 1914, Vanderlip
Collection.

for example, felt a severe contraction in unfinished orders from 7.8 million tons in January 1913 to 4.3 million tons in December 1913.[4]

Pressure for an American branch banking system developed very rapidly, and by June 1914 Vanderlip was asking Stillman's permission to proceed. For months, Pierre S. DuPont, treasurer of the E. I. du Pont Nemours Powder Company, a firm with extensive interests in Chilean nitrates, had been pushing Vanderlip to become active in South America.[5] James A. Farrell, who had attained the presidency of the United States Steel Corporation by vigorously developing its export sales division, told Vanderlip that his corporation had extensive plans for extending its $100 million a year export business as soon as the Federal suit against the big trust was settled. He urged Vanderlip to go ahead with the branch bank operation. "The time is absolutely right," he said, "for the City Bank to establish a branch in Rio and one in Buenos Aires and later a few more."[6] He promised Vanderlip that U. S. Steel would

---

[4] William C. Schluter, The Pre-War Business Cycle, 1907 to 1914, published dissertation of Columbia University (New York: 1923), pp. 127 - 183. Also Friedman and Schwartz, A Monetary History of the United States (Princeton: Princeton University Press, 1963), p. 174.

[5] John Gardin to Vanderlip, 15 February 1914, Vanderlip Coll.

[6] Vanderlip to James Stillman, 5 June 1914, Vanderlip Coll.

cooperate in every way, giving the bank access to its existing credit files and keeping its deposits with City.

As head of the National Foreign Trade Council, and in other ways familiar with export trends, Farrell also assured Vanderlip that International Harvester, Swift and Armour would also turn to City to handle their foreign business.[7] Those corporations, and others of the same size, supplied 75 per cent of United States exports to Latin America. Vanderlip himself felt more sanguine about the development, particularly since the difficulty of getting men with the right training which had troubled him in previous years, had, at least "in some measure," been solved. He consequently proposed to Stillman "a modest trial of South American banking" and planned to present the Federal Reserve Board with an application from the City Bank for a branch in Buenos Aires. "Then," he added, "we could go to the merchants and offer them credit information and representation." He did not immediately expect big profits from the branches but the home office, he predicted, "would at

---

[7]Ibid., and William H. Lough, Banking Opportunities in South America, Department of Commerce, Bureau of Foreign and Domestic Commerce, Special Agent Series No. 106 (Washington, 1905), p. 135.

once begin to show a profit" through new accounts in
the United States.[8]

The outbreak of World War I in August 1914 sharply
intensified the recession and the desire of manufacturers
and merchants for an American foreign banking system.
British banks buying exchange on South America and
otherwise assisting in the conduct of world commerce
in normal times temporarily ceased these operations,
and that made it impossible to negotiate drafts on
London banks for the South American trade and world trade
in general. The method of financing through England
had collapsed.[9] That crisis, along with the shipping

[8]Vanderlip to Stillman, 5 June 1915, Vanderlip Coll.
Also see Chapter One, supra and Records of the Board of
Governors of the Federal Reserve System, Federal Deposit
Insurance Building, Washington, D. C. (FRB) 421.2 (1-12),
Benjamin Strong (chairman, New York Federal Reserve
Bank) to Paul Warburg (member, Federal Reserve Board),
28 October 1915. Strong wrote that NCB officers had
told him more than once that profits from foreign
branches would be comparatively small for years to come;
that the immediate profit would arise from increased
domestic business growing out of the establishment of
the branches for the bank's customers who were engaged
in foreign trade.

[9]Secretary of State William J. Bryan to Secretary
of Treasury William G. McAdoo, 25 August 1914, Box 121,
McAdoo Papers, Library of Congress. William E. Peck
and Co. had supplied Bryan with the information. See
also Frank E. Hagemeyer (Hagemeyer Trading Co., New
York City) to McAdoo, 2 September 1914, Box 122, McAdoo
Papers, L.C. Telegrams from State Department consuls
reported that banks in South America refused to buy or
sell foreign exchange and recommended the establishment
of American banks. NARS, RG 59, 811.516/29, 30 and
NARS, RG 56, Stenographic Report of a Conference held
at the Treasury Department, etc., 14 August 1914, p. 60.

difficulties and the already depressed condition of the economy, brought cries of anguish from the business community.

Secretary of the Treasury William Gibbs McAdoo immediately called a conference at Washington of the nations' most important banking and commercial leaders. After considerable discussion, much of it revealing the ignorance of American commercial men on questions of foreign exchange and finance, the Secretary succeeded in creating a committee of representative bankers to work on the problem with Paul M. Warburg of the Federal Reserve Board.[10] This foreign exchange committee recommended that, in lieu of a discount system market on Federal Reserve Bank purchases, the Secretary of the Treasury should deposit Treasury funds in financial institutions that would employ those funds in purchasing American bills of exchange issued against shipments of commodities, especially foodstuffs, to Europe. The Treasury quickly implemented this suggestion and New York banks began discounting bills of dollar exchange, mostly against London, with Treasury funds. The committee also suggested the Federal Reserve Board study the question of having the United States government cooperate

---

[10]NARS, RG56, Stenographic Report, 14 August 1914, pp. 83, 91.

with the governments of Europe in setting up an international clearing house to ease the strain on the
astronomical rates for foreign exchange.[11]

The financial community closed the stock exchange
in anticipation of British liquidation of American
securities and braced itself for a severe drain on its
gold reserves as Great Britain prepared to demand payment on all due debts. To forestall the worst effects
of this development, McAdoo invited Sir George Paish
and Sir Basil Blackett of the British Exchequer to New
York.[12] At the same time, an unofficial delegation of
American bankers including Henry P. Davison (Morgan &
Company) and James Brown (Brown Brothers) sailed for
London and discussions with British financial leaders.

A damaging drain on the United States' gold supply
through excessive demands by creditors could only
curtail American credit and hurt England. Sir George
Paish therefore agreed that, if British withdrawal of
gold threatened American banks reserves, the Bank of
England would accept payment of American deficits in
the form of finance bills (really short term unsecured
loans) and would not object, upon their maturity, to

---

[11]Warburg to McAdoo, 18 August 1914, McAdoo
Papers, Box 121, Library of Congress.

[12]Charles Hamlin Diary, Volume 2, 24 October 1914,
Hamlin Collection, Library of Congress.

payment in other forms of credit.[13] Still later, in
December 1914, when it became clear that America's
favorable trade position made its financial position
exceptionally strong, an informal arrangement with London provided for a mutual reciprocal credit. If exchange
became adverse to New York, and if gold had been shipped
to the danger line, a credit would be established in
London. The reverse procedure would be followed if
British reserves seemed in jeopardy.[14] London approved
the informal plan in conference with Davison and Brown,
"not only because of benefit in operation possible
future need of which is doubted /because England had

---

[13]Ibid. For use of the Treasury funds for dis-
counting see McAdoo to A. J. Hemphill (Guaranty Trust
Company), 19 August 1914, McAdoo Papers, Library of
Congress.

[14]American obligations at the outbreak of the war
totaled $500 million, $200 million of which was due by
1 January 1915. George Reynolds, "The Effect of the
European War on American Credits," Journal of Political
Economy, Vol. 22, p. 931. For an outline of the agreement see Federal Record Center (FRC) Arlington,
Virginia, RG 39, Box 101, New York Federal Reserve
Bank Correspondence. These records were copied from
the files of the Bank by the Nye Committee. Most of
them are reproduced in the Hearings of the Special
Committee Investigating the Munitions Industry, 74th
Congress, 2nd Session (Washington, 1936). Henry P.
Davison to /J. P. Morgan7, 9 December 1914. Davison
made it clear that the delegation to London had acted
unofficially and that it was futile to set up the plan
immediately. But there was no question in his mind as
to the formation of such a syndicate should an emer-
gency arise. For consummation of the deal see
Chapter III.

ample supplies of American securities to cash in7 but
because of excellent sentimental effect."[15]   This
marked the beginning of a process that created American-
British financial interdependence.   It was a development
of impressive, seemingly inevitable, smoothness and
cordiality.

Wartime relations with Latin America opened with
characteristic improvisation.   Congress wanted to dis-
patch, "at least six naval vessels to the principal
ports of South America, with samples of manufactures
and products of the United States together with business
organization representatives," and was dissuaded only
by the Secretary of Commerce's explanation that the
basis of trade would have to be credits which the United
States was not yet prepared to extend.[16]   The Congres-
sional spasm was understandable and not really unusual
considering the American orientation towards the
southern half of the hemisphere.   Latin America had
already become an important outlet for American products,
and it had been cut off by the disruption of financial,
and to some extent, shipping facilities.[17]   In the first

---

[15]Ibid.

[16]NARS, RG 40, 72155/17, Secretary of Commerce
William Redfield to James M. Baker (Secretary of the
Senate), 16 September 1914.

[17]Total U. S. exports to Latin America in 1914
valued $309 million, approximately 12 per cent of the
total value of American exports. U. S. Bureau of the

months of the crisis, when the nation confronted a depression, the Wilson Administration attacked these
problems with desperate energy. Moreover, South
America represented a market of great potential, opening to untrammeled American development while Britain
turned its resources to combat. For, paradoxically,
Britain was weakened even as it controlled the shipping
routes and terminated, at least temporarily, German
operations in Latin America. American weakness in
finance and shipping precluded complete capture of this
market, but the prospective sharing of it with England,
to the exclusion of Germany, immediately became one of
the unspoken understandings of the war.[18]

Less than a month after the war started, the
Secretaries of State and Commerce organized a conference bringing together Latin American diplomatic
representatives and men from American business. The

Census, Historical Statistics of the United States,
Colonial Times to 1957, (Washington, D. C., 1960),
p. 550.

[18]A writer for the New York Times observed in 1915
that England was mistress of the seas and that our
whole policy was based on the assumption of the friend-
liness of England and upon the belief "that England
will not attack us and will on the contrary defend
us." New York Times, 5 December 1915, VIII, p. 4. In
late 1916, the British Ambassador to the United States,
Sir Cecil Spring-Rice, told a member of the Federal
Reserve Board that he hoped that the United States
would get all the South American trade which formerly
went to Germany. Hamlin Diary, 30 December 1916,
Volume 4, Library of Congress.

economic leaders included those from commercial and
industrial organizations, the Chamber of Commerce of
the United States, The Southern Commercial Congress,
and the National Foreign Trade Council. The meeting
appointed a Latin American Trade Commission headed by
James A. Farrell and Robert H. Patchin (Grace & Co.),
and adopted the recommendations of the vociferously
expansionist National Foreign Trade Council on Latin
American trade.[19] Continued reliance on the British
banking system, they argued, would give England a free
hand in appropriating for itself, and at American
expense, Germany's position in Latin America while
American goods, for lack of credits, remained "congested
on our docks" until British credit again became available.

"An attempt should now be made," the conference
declared, "to evolve some plan whereby we might take
advantage of our large direct trade with Latin America
to make a market for bills drawn in dollars, and establish a direct exchange, not with the view to eliminating
sterling credits now or later, but in order to provide
an exchange channel which will supplement, offset, or

---

[19]U. S. Senate, 63rd Congress, 3rd Session, Doc.
No. 714, Report of the Latin American Trade Committee (Washington, 1915), p. 4.

compete with London and be available when London
exchange is disorganized."[20]   Concluding that the
cessation of trade with Latin America would be highly
injurious to American industry, and that the extension
of this trade would contribute to the prosperity of
the country at large, the Commission recommended that
the Federal Reserve Board immediately begin the discounting operations provided for in the Federal Reserve
Act, and thereby lay the groundwork for an American
trade finance system.[21]

The National City Bank thus enjoyed a most auspi-
cious climate to initiate foreign expansion. No sooner
had it declared its intention of opening branches in
South America in July 1914 than hundreds of letters
began pouring into its offices each day, commending the
institution for its decision. Deposits and accounts
increased steadily, and the work of the foreign exchange
division assumed great proportions.[22] Without a rediscount market, however, the bank's discount bills of
exchange against New York locked up reserves and
severely limited the amount of credit that could be

---

[20]Ibid., p. 20.

[21]Ibid., p. 11.

[22]Vanderlip to Ruth Harden, 3 July 1914, Vanderlip
Collection, and Vanderlip to Stillman, 9 October 1914,
Vanderlip Collection.

extended. The opening of the Federal Reserve Banks in
November released about $480 million previously held as
reserves by member banks and also provided a rediscount
market for dollar bills of exchange.[23] In the same
month, National City opened branches in Buenos Aires,
Argentina, offering six months credit in acceptances
for drafts drawn against New York, and extensive commercial connections to importers, exporters, and
manufacturers in the United States.

With customary European capital exports disrupted,
the Bank's opening seemed a significant and hopeful sign
to capital-starved Latin Americans. To clarify the
force of its intention and create a favorable impression throughout the continent, the Bank floated a
$15 million loan for the Republic of Argentina in
December 1914.[24] In New York, Vanderlip accepted some

---

[23]George Reynolds, op. cit., p. 936.

[24]A study of South American finance made before the
war broke out by Edward N. Hurley indicated that
Brazilians, at least, did not think of the United
States as a first rate power because of apparent
financial weakness. The Argentine loan was expected
to overcome this view and promote cooperation with
American foreign banks. U. S. Senate, 63rd Congress,
3rd Session, Doc. No. 659, Banking and Credit in
Argentina, Brazil, Chile, and Peru (Washington, 1914),
p. 51. The Argentines had also asked England for the
loan but, the Times observed, foreign money markets
were practically closed to all but home financing.
New York Times, 2 January 1915, p. 10. Previous
American participations in foreign loan flotations (and
there had been quite a few) had been possible only

additional accounts for his bank and the congratulations
of Charles Schwab, the steel magnate, who felt that City
alone 'had the nerve to do business of this kind which
was absolutely essential to the business of the country."[25]
Vanderlip had chosen "the psychological moment, for the
American entré into an investment field previously
dominated by understandings among European financiers."
Though he had no illusions about New York's becoming
"the financial center of the world," Vanderlip readily
acknowledged that, "with complete disorganization of
the world's exchanges we are going to play a very important part."[26]

As Vanderlip had earlier anticipated, the depressed
conditions in Latin America reduced the chronically

---

because the loans were redeemable in foreign currencies
as well as in American dollars. This gave American
investors the assurance that they could always sell
their participation on some European bourse. The
National City Argentine loan of 1915 was redeemable in
dollars alone and therefore signified a certain coming
of age of American finance. Large banks in New York,
Boston, Chicago, Pittsburgh, and Philadelphia bought
participations. New York Times, 1 January 1915, p. 10.
C. V. Rich (vice-president NCB) wrote James Stillman
that the Bank's purpose in handling the loan was to create a favorable impression in South America to the
National City Bank and its branches, 11 December 1914,
Vanderlip Collection. The Argentines thought the rate
excessive but had no other recourse. December 1914,
Edward Currier (Vanderlip's Secretary) to Vanderlip,
Vanderlip Collection.

[25]Ibid., 6 January 1915.

[26]Vanderlip to Stillman, 9 October 1914, Vanderlip
Collection.

inflated values and increased the attractiveness of
investment prices. This factor, together with the
prospect of increasing trade and the fear of imminent
American competition, convinced the bank to modify its
conservative policy and "go ahead" early in 1915. It
moved to "take advantage of the world-wide readjustment
of business."[27] Herbert R. Eldridge, a vice president
of the bank touring the Latin America, reported that
the future of the branch bank business was "immense...
much greater than I had any conception of when I left
New York."[28] The Federal Reserve Board quickly granted
permission for a branch in Rio (with sub-branches in
Sao Paulo and Santos), and for one in Havana with sub-
branches throughout Cuba and in Santo Domingo and
Jamaica.[29] The bank allocated about $1,000,000 for
each branch; the sub-branches merely functioned as
agencies without separate capital.

When Paul Warburg proposed the creation of a separate branch (rather than a sub-branch) in Montevideo as

[27]This was the judgment of Herbert R. Eldridge,
a vice president of NCB. Edward P. Currier to Vanderlip, 28 June 1915, Vanderlip Collection.

[28]Ibid., 4 October 1915.

[29]FRB 421.2-24, Warburg to Frederic A. Delano
(then vice governor of the Federal Reserve Board,
1 April 1915.

befitting the state pride of "so large a country as
Uruguay," the Bank, in effect, refused. By way of explanation, vice president William S. Kies revealed the
nature of City's commitment to Latin America:

> The City Bank is endeavoring to give banking
> facilities in foreign markets where needed.
> It is not desirable to apportion too much
> capital to South America. Branches are needed
> on the West coast, and in Venezuela and
> Colombia, and, if it is determined to
> establish branches in those places, probably
> one and a half million dollars will have to be
> set aside for those banks. Considering the
> West Indies as a part of South America, this
> will mean four and one-half million dollars
> capital set aside for the doing of business
> in South America.[30]

That was too much, at least in the bank's opinion. For
that matter, the branches were not expected to take
capital indefinitely from the home office for their
development, but rather to extend their operations with
deposits from the host country.[31]

Vanderlip had genuine but not unlimited optimism
for the future of the National City Bank in South
America. But those prospects were small compared with

---

[30]Kies accounted this a more important argument
against the establishment of a branch in Uruguay than
the fact that the amount of business in Uruguay did not
warrant the establishment of a branch. Kies to M. C.
Elliot (counsel for the Federal Reserve Board),
6 April 1915. In 1917, the NCB sub-branch at Montevideo was made into a full branch.

[31]See footnote 38.

other projects he planned for the future. The most
notable of those was the development of ties with
Russia, where the war had created a market free of
traditional German dominance. "I doubt whether there
is any field one part as fertile as this," he remarked
of Russia, and planned to begin with short term
credit that would "develop business in America."[32]
From that point, he expected the business to "grow into
many channels" - the prospect of investments being
foremost - but including City Bank branches in Paris and
London. "That ought to bring us a great deal of new
business," he speculated, "especially after such credit
information as we will be able to give when we are in
full swing."[33] Discrete but firm exercise of power
would sufficiently assuage French and English interests
which, rightly or wrongly, regarded the field as
theirs.[34]

Before the war ended, the City representative in
Russia, H. Fessenden Meserve, had opened a Petrograd

[32]C. V. Rich (vice president NCB) to Vanderlip,
9 June 1916, Vanderlip Collection. Also Vanderlip to
H. F. Meserve, 28 April 1917, Vanderlip Collection.

[33]C. V. Rich to Vanderlip, 7 July 1916, Vanderlip
Collection.

[34]Rich to Vanderlip, 9 June 1916, Vanderlip Col-
lection. For the importance of the German's absence see
Samuel McRoberts (vice president NCB) address before the
U. S. Chamber of Commerce, 3 February 1915, "Our National
Policy as to Investments Abroad." Unbound pamphlet.

branch; and it became self-supporting on the income
from Russian Treasury bills in which the Bank had
invested during the course of the war. There were also
hopes to open a branch in Moscow. Unsettled conditions
made comparatively small dollar credits in high demand
among influential Russian companies, which in normal
times would have had little interest in opening an
account with an American bank. Meserve, aware of the
prime commercial importance of Moscow, was alert to the
need for early action.[35] Events beyond City's control
thwarted those ambitions.

The bank's move into the Orient unfurled in a
single swoop with the purchase of the International
Banking Corporation from Morgan and Kuhn, Loeb. I. B. C.
had specialized in financing trade with China (in sterling) after 1901, when it was created to assist the
United States government in the collection of the Boxer
indemnity. The Shangai office was opened in 1902. The
Peking, Hankow, and Tientsin offices were opened a few
years later with the explicit purpose of assisting the
American consortium just formed for purposes of
reorganizing Chinese finance.[36] The China trade was

---

[35]H. F. Meserve to Vanderlip, 23 February 1917,
Vanderlip Collection.

[36]Federal Reserve Bulletin, 1 October 1916, p. 945.
Federal Reserve Bulletin, 1 October 1918, p. 945. Clyde

so linked with other Eastern countries that branches in
Japan, the Straits Settlements and India followed. It
then moved into Panama as an aid to the United States
government in the construction of the Panama Canal, and
in Santo Domingo.

The I. B. C. dealt in dollar exchange and sterling
through a branch in London and concentrated on financing
trade between Asian ports. When City purchased it,
I. B. C. had 15 branches in the Orient, and in the next
10 years established 19 additional branches in the
Caribbean and Far East.[37] National City Bank's foreign
branches had by 1916 drawn over $12 million in credit
from the home office funds which otherwise would have
idled in the vaults. Contrary to expectations, all the
branches produced profits.[38] Vanderlip was impressed

W. Phelps, _The Foreign Expansion of American Banks_
(Ronald Press: 1927), p. 147. Considering the size
and importance of the I. B. C., I am somewhat embar-
rassed to be able to say no more about it than this.

[37]Federal Reserve Bulletin, 1 October 1918, p. 945.
Phelps, _op. cit._, p. 144. In 1916, the NCB bought a
controlling interest in the Banque Nationale de la Repub-
lique d'Haiti through its subsidiary the National City
Company. The war made it necessary for an American
committee to take charge and German stockholders sold
out their interest. _New York Times_, 7 July 1916, p. 14.

[38]NCB Foreign Department memo to Vanderlip,
4 April 1916, Vanderlip Collection, and _Ibid._, 10 October 1916. NCB Foreign Department accounts grew as
follows: 534(1913), 822(1914), 1347(1915), 2120(1916),
2901(1917), 3246(1918 January-June). Deposits in South
America grew from $2,323,091.21 in 1915 to $4,322,675.58

with the tremendous increase in exports and, more importantly, with the development of the willingness of
American manufacturers to respond to specific foreign
demands for every and any kind of manufacturers.[39]

Favored by these circumstances and arrangements,
the National City Bank soon gained a unique position
in the Latin American trade. More than 80 per cent of
the nation's South American commerce passed through
New York even though much of it originated in the
interior.[40] The shipping documents were completed and
the goods, if imported, were received in New York; and
all the related factors, such as commission houses,
shipping agents, and foreign exchange houses of the
import-export trade were consolidated there. The 21
banks seriously enough involved in foreign trade to
maintain foreign exchange departments were mainly
interested in dealing with Europe.[41] A few had

---

in 1916. Total world deposits of the bank in 1916 were
$144,269,783.74. Of this, $126,999,943.52 were drawn
from 1170 accounts in Europe. Foreign Department memo
to Vanderlip 19 October 1915, Vanderlip Collection, and
FRB 332.314(2), Warburg to Federal Reserve Board,
23 November 1916 (enclosure). Funds drawn by the South
American branches increased to $12,000,000 by 1917.

[39]Vanderlip's foreign trade statistician pointed
out the significance of the developments. O. P. Austin
to Vanderlip, 23 September 1916, Vanderlip Collection.

[40]Lough, op. cit., p. 145-146.

[41]Ibid., p. 146. The Guaranty Trust had established
a London branch in 1897 and another in London and one

long-range connections, through European correspondents, with South America.

Under these circumstances, Edward N. Hurley, a midwestern manufacturer who was also a Wilsonian Progressive and militant expansionist, and who served as vice-chairman of the Federal Trade Commission, concluded in 1915 that unless an American manufacturer had an account with the National City Bank in New York he would have a poor chance of getting in touch with Argentinian buyers.[42] Hurley cared most about western manufacturers who had no direct connections with any foreign bank. Many of them were opening accounts with City, "but the small manufacturer who cannot justify carrying two accounts, is at a great disadvantage because he must maintain his local credit connections." Hurley, anticipating City's further development, observed to the

in Paris in 1916. The Equitable Trust Company and the Farmers Trust Company both had branches in London and Paris before the war. The latter was closely associated with the NCB. Phelps, op. cit., pp. 133-140.

[42]NARS, RG40, 72155/33, Edward N. Hurley to William Redfield, 25 May 1915. Hurley was very concerned with foreign expansion. Some of the refinements of his approach may be measured by his remark that if American industries surrendered potential markets to their competitors, they would contribute to profits that would enable their competitors to incur losses in their efforts to invade the U. S. commercially. He concluded that the development of foreign trade was a necessary defensive as well as an offensive operation in international commerce. See his Banking and Credit in Argentina etc., p. 66.

Secretary of Commerce, William C. Redfield, "unless the
Chicago and other Middle Western bankers are permitted
to cooperate in organizing foreign branch banks, the
National City Bank will soon be controlling not only
American banking in the foreign countries in which they
have opened branches, but they will also be controlling
the market of the countries in which their banks are
located."[43]

Redfield thought the development of American
foreign trade the single most important task of his
department, and naturally viewed with alarm the potential
control of that trade by a single bank. Immediately
after the war began, his agents studied financial
opportunities at home and abroad to smooth the way for
efficient development of American commercial finance.
As early as November 23, 1914, they planned a conference
of American bankers "to supplant the foreign financial
interests... with an American financial interest which
would be less selfish and more useful in developing
both Latin America and our own commerce."[44] Redfield
was supported by most American bankers in that objective, but none -- with the exception of the National

---

[43]NARS, RG40, 72155/33, Hurley to Redfield, 25 May
1915.

[44]NARS, RG40, 72155/33, Redfield to Secretary of
State Bryan, 23 November 1914.

City Bank -- were equipped to undertake such a financial
struggle. Boston bankers conceded this point before
the war, and declined the Commerce Department's invita-
tion to establish a bank in Chile "because it would not
prove to be a paying one for a Boston bank and also
because of the reported intention of the National City
Bank of New York to establish a branch there."[45]

Both of the big Boston national banks, the National
Shawmut and the First National, expressed their readiness, however, to combine with other banks and establish
branches not only in Chile but in other South American
countries.[46] This reinforced Hurley's conclusion, and
Redfield passed the Boston reply on to Charles S. Hamlin
(Governor of the Federal Reserve Board), Secretary
McAdoo, and President Wilson. A Commerce Department
agent reported that leading bankers in St. Louis and
New Orleans, as well as those in Chicago and New York,
were willing to take part in any practical plan of cooperation in the organization of foreign banks. They
concluded that there was no reason to doubt that a

---

[45]FRB 421.2, F. L. Roberts (Bureau of Domestic and
Foreign Commerce) to E. E. Pratt (chief of bureau),
29 March 1915.

[46]Ibid. Hurley had also recommended a provision
allowing national banks to cooperate. For evidence of
FTC, Commerce, and FRB cooperation in this matter see
NARS, RG40, Redfield to Hurley, 7 June 1915, 72155/33
and Ibid., 72155/33, Redfield to Charles Hamlin,
6 April 1915.

cooperative venture could be easily organized "once
Congress amended the National Bank Act to allow the
national banks to combine in a joint venture."[47] The
Board of Governors of the Federal Reserve System
appeared very favorable to the project, but preferred
for the initiative to come from the bankers. Paul Warburg told the Commerce Department agent that "the
establishment and development of such banks is of the
highest importance for the commercial interests of this
country," and suggested that the bankers go ahead and
get up a plan and submit it to Congress.[48]

Secretary of the Treasury McAdoo had other plans.
He blocked the Commerce Department's plans for an
informal meeting with the bankers, preferring to delay
that step and merge it with his own Pan-American
Financial Conference scheduled for the middle of the
year. McAdoo wanted the conference to bring American
and Latin American business interests together to discuss
the creation of dollar exchange, the extension of better
credit facilities, and the establishment of branch banks
before large public gatherings designed to furnish
general information about the new American financial

---

[47]NARS, RG40, 72155/33, W. M. Lough memo for Redfield, 9 January 1915.

[48]Ibid.

44

mechanism.[49] Small private committee meetings would
enable specially interested manufacturers and financiers to meet with representatives of individual Latin
nations to discuss the financing of internal development. When the Conference ended, having excited
considerable interest in South America, McAdoo advanced
his own plan for American financial expansion in a
report to President Wilson.

McAdoo rejected the FTC-Commerce plan, which had
been supported by several leading bankers at the Conference, that Congress amend the National Bank Act to
permit national banks to become stockholders in independent banks organized to do business abroad.[50]
Instead, he suggested that the Federal Reserve Banks,
which included in their membership every national bank
in the United States as well as a number of the leading
state banks and trust companies, establish agencies
abroad to finance American trade and other operations
in the various countries in which they would operate.[51]
The Federal Reserve Act gave the banks of the system

[49]NARS, RG40, 72155, McAdoo to Redfield, 11 May
1915.

[50]FRB 301.2, McAdoo to Hamlin, 7 August 1915.

[51]Ibid., and Report of Secretary of Treasury,
6 September, to the President on the Recent Pan-
American Financial Conference, quoted in the Federal
Reserve Bulletin, Volume 1, 1915, p. 313.

the power to establish such agencies; and, although it
did not require them to do so, he argued that "upon a
careful study of the situation and with the encouragement of the Federal Reserve Board, they will be prompted
to take this important step."[52] President Wilson, who
relied very closely on McAdoo for advice in financial
policy, endorsed the recommendations. "These suggestions meet with my entire approval and I hope that it
will be possible to carry out so promising a plan. It
ought to be fruitful of the most desirable results.
May I suggest that you bring the plan to the attention
of the Federal Reserve Board and enlist, if possible,
their cooperation."[53]

The Federal Reserve Board, interested in preserving
the foreign business for the bankers and distrustful of
the financial wisdom of McAdoo's scheme, was preparing
a long report refuting his position when McAdoo published the President's letter. Already smouldering
over unsettled questions regarding its status in the
government bureaucracy and its degree of responsibility
to the Secretary of the Treasury, the Board repudiated
McAdoo's position in what newspapers construed as a

---

[52]Ibid.

[53]FRB 301.2, Woodrow Wilson to McAdoo (copy),
5 October 1915.

direct slap at the Secretary and the President.[54] In

a long press statement, the Board pointed out that the

Federal Reserve Banks, being properly restricted by law

from engaging in credit business which risked their

absolute liquidity, could never compete with German,

French, and English independent banks of deposit in

Latin America.

"The contribution of the Federal Reserve Banks in

this development of Latin America," the Board argued,

"should primarily consist in providing conditions so

favorable for American acceptances that the American

banks willing to offer credit facilities there will be

materially assisted in meeting the European rates which,

at the present time and probably for some time to come

will compare unfavorably with the American discount

rate."[55] The Board recommended an amendment to the

Federal Reserve Act that would enable American member

banks to cooperate for the purpose of jointly owning

and operating foreign banks. The committee took the

position that American banks entering the foreign field

ought to be permitted to develop the opportunities first

but that, in trade centers where American bankers were

[54]Hamlin Diary, Volume 3, 8 October 1915, Library
of Congress.

[55]Federal Reserve Bulletin, Volume 1, 1915, p. 348.
Copy of the press statement issued by the Board,
12 October 1915.

not established, the Federal Reserve Banks as empowered
by the Act might appoint agents to deal in foreign
exchange for the purpose of encouraging the development
of dollar exchange. Under pressure from the major
financial communities of the country, McAdoo yielded
to the Board's position with the result that the
amendment permitting such affiliations was passed by
the Congress in 1916.[56]

Consequently, young Hayden Harris of Harris Forbes
& Co. organized under New York laws the American Foreign
Banking Corporation, through which a number of national
banks throughout the country (the most prominent ones
being in Boston, Philadelphia, St. Louis, Cleveland,
Chicago, and New Orleans) pooled $5,000,000 for the
purposes of establishing branches or of buying into
existing banks in South America and elsewhere.[57] The
corporation had several advantages over the National

---

[56]The Advisory Council, The Federal Reserve Agents,
and the Conference of Governors were in agreement
against McAdoo's plan. FRB 301.2, Warburg memo for the
Federal Reserve Board, 8 January 1916. Also FRB 301.2,
James B. Forgan to C. H. Bosworth (chairman Federal
Reserve Bank, Chicago) 6 December 1915, and FRB 421.2
(1-12), D. C. Willis (chairman Federal Reserve Bank,
Cleveland) to H. Parker Willis (Secretary to Federal
Reserve Board) 14 December 1915.

[57]FRB, 421.2, Pierre Jay (Federal Reserve Agent,
New York) to Warburg, 2 April 1917. NARS, RG59,
812.51/318, 14 August 1917 for a list of stockholders.
Also Phelps, op. cit., p. 156. For another list of
stockholders see FRB 421.2-7, passim.

City system. Foreign countries, for example, taxed only the capital of the corporation, not the capital of the banks. Also, membership in a corporate entity limited the liability of stockholders to their original investment. But the law prevented the corporation from accepting deposits in the United States unless they were directly connected with foreign trade. This effectively forced the corporation to go overseas for additional operating capital.[58]

The Bank made its initial efforts in Brazilian rubber, which was then engaged in fierce competition with the British crop from Southeast Asia. The corporation also backed Haitian coffee in a price struggle with the Brazilian brand by financing the crop and selling it through its own distributors in New York. If the market failed to absorb the crop in 90 days, the banks issued a straight long term loan to the distributor on the security of the coffee in order to complete payments to the shipper in Haiti.[59] The Bank had established 19 branches by 1920. Most of them were in South and Central America, but it had one in China and one in the Philippine Islands.[60]

---

[58]FRB 421.2-7, Archibald Kains (president) to Warburg, 10 August 1917.

[59]NARS, RG59, 832.516/7, R. Mommsen (American vice consul at Rio) to Lansing, 5 January 1918. RG59, 838,61333/11.

[60]Phelps, op. cit., p. 156.

In the meantime, private bankers led by Brown
Brothers and J. W. Seligman & Co. of New York launched
a third foreign bank network. They pooled $5,000,000
and organized the Mercantile Bank of the Americas, to
buy control of local banks in South and Central America,
and to create affiliated trading corporations in each
country. The Mercantile Bank held the controlling share
of stock in each operation.[61] The enterprise grew out
of the developing foreign interest of Brown Brothers
and Seligman after their takeover of the National Bank
of Nicaragua with State Department support in 1912.
The new Mercantile Bank owned 51 per cent of that bank,
which was the sole source of issue for Nicaragua.[62]
Mercantile chartered the Mercantile Bank of Peru in
June 1916, and the entire $500,000 stock was owned by
Mercantile. Its purpose was to finance trade between
Peru and the United States, and it was planned that a
small share in the operation would later be sold to
prominent Peruvians.[63] Both the Nicaraguan and Peruvian
banks financed long term loans in the host countries
from local deposits. The Mercantile Bank itself did

---

[61]FRB 421/2-16, no date, unsigned, memo to Board
on operation of Mercantile Bank of Americas on
company stationery.

[62]Ibid.

[63]Ibid.

not extend any capital except for purposes of financing
imports or exports at short term.[64]

The Bank also chartered the Mercantile Overseas
Corporation in July 1916 in order to hold commercial
properties, to make commandite banking arrangements with
existing local institutions, and to function as a trading company when primitive economic conditions dictated.
In Columbia, for example, the Corporation worked with
an organization owned by Columbia Railways and Navi-
gations Company, Limited (London) which controlled about
60 per cent of the transportation on the Magialena
River, the main artery of commerce in Columbia. Under
the terms, the branches of the bank used all the
facilities of all the branches and subsidiaries of the
British firm and in return participated in the profits
and losses of all its banking and commercial business
in Columbia.[65] In addition, the Bank had a branch in
Ecuador heavily committed to financing the cocoa trade.

Within three years after the passage of the
Federal Reserve Act, American banks had committed
approximately $22 million to the establishment and
actual operation of three distinct foreign banking
systems. One was the one created by the National City

---

[64]Ibid.

[65]Ibid.

Bank, which seemed at the outset to represent the
largest corporations and many smaller firms from all
over the country. The second was headed by the Mercantile Bank of the Americas and composed of the private
bankers. The third was the American Foreign Banking
Corporation sponsored by the smaller national banks.
All three followed established banking practice. They
sought to draw on local deposits for their operations
and to diversify their interests. Partly by chance
and partly by design, they entered the business at a
time when the Latin American depression created a
propitious climate for acquiring assets, and they were
supported by a business community increasingly aware of
the importance of foreign markets to the national
economy. All these factors helped to make them successful.

This establishment of American foreign branch
banks represented only a part of the foreign expansion
of American banking that followed the passage of the
Federal Reserve Act. The new acceptance facilities
provided for the National Banks facilitated a greatly
increased use of dollar exchange in international commerce. This was especially true in South America,
where all the German banks (and even some English)
began to rely on New York to accept their endorsed

bills of exchange.[66] In this way, a large number of
banks in New York, Boston, and Philadelphia used their
acceptance powers to extend credit in dollars to the
international economy. As early as April 1915, for
example, New York banks alone had created acceptance
liabilities of $80-$100 million.[67]

As the war strait-jacketed British trade and reduced the amount of European capital available for
trade finance, dollar exchange made steady encroachments
on the sterling empire. At the same time, the amount
of foreign business transacted on government order by
the British Treasury sharply reduced the volume of
commercial sterling bills handled by the London market.
Even so, the financial pressure on British banks was
such that by 1916 they began to recommend the use of
dollar bills of exchange to their regular commercial
customers.[68] American banks financed the American and
Egyptian cotton crop to England with bills drawn in
dollars against British importers. The use of dollar
exchange in the Far East increased with the growing

[66]New York Federal Reserve Bank (NYFRB), Strong
Correspondence, Strong to Franklin Locke, 23 October 1916.

[67]NYFRB, File 440, Strong to Franklin Locke,
5 April 1915.

[68]NYFRB, Strong Correspondence, Strong to Warburg,
11 September 1916. See also Kenzel to Strong,
29 August 1916.

American trade in jute and silk, and that in turn created a growing reliance by British foreign banks on
American acceptance power. Sir Edward Holden, head of
the powerful and expansionist London City and Midland
Bank, publicly wept over what he feared was the passing
of sterling supremacy.[69] On the other hand, Sir
Charles Addis, chairman of the important and reputable
Hong Kong and Shanghai Banking Corporation, was enthusiastic. He told Benjamin Strong, and most English
bankers agreed with him, that New York must carry some
of the load for financing the world's commerce.[70]

The Federal Reserve Board further increased the
use of dollar exchange in 1916 by obtaining from the
Congress an amendment to the Federal Reserve Act that
allowed American banks to accept bills of exchange in
dollars that were used to finance trade between nations
other than the United States. This facilitated the
replacement of sterling with dollars as the medium of
exchange between South America and Europe.[71] As a

---

[69]Federal Records Center (FRC), Arlington, Virginia, Record Group 39, World War I records, Box 101,
James Brown to Benjamin Strong, 4 August 1916.

[70]NYFRB, Strong Diary, 13 March 1916, record of
conversation with Sir Charles Addis.

[71]Federal Reserve Bulletin, 1 December 1916, p. 665.
FRC Arlington, RG39, Box 101, Warburg to Senator Robert
L. Owen, 11 May 1916. Also, Warburg, The Federal
Reserve System, Volume 2, p. 418. The Board also

result, shipments of merchandise from Holland to Argentina, for example, and of coffee from Brazil to Italy, were financed in dollars. By the end of 1916, New York banks had acceptance liabilities in the neighborhood of $150 million; all of America's banks held between $200 and $250 million.[72] And, as more and more bills called for settlement in dollars, the foreign exchange markets of most countries began to quote the going rates for dollar exchange.

In spite of the numerous signs of a burgeoning American acceptance business after the establishment of the Federal Reserve System, several obstacles blocked its development. While the war accelerated the use of dollar exchange, that development occurred in an abnormal way. The war made the United States the major world source of capital and goods. British wartime restrictions on trade drove many foreign businessmen to the American market, even prompting them to exchange their sterling assets for dollars in London.[73] But American manufacturers displayed limited attitudes toward

increased national banks acceptance power to 100 per cent of capital surplus, Annual Report, Federal Reserve Board, 1916, p. 4.

[72]NYFRB, File 440, HPA / ? / to Strong, 27 March 1917. Also NYFRB, File 440, Strong to Robert Treman (director, NYFRB), 11 January 1917.

[73]New York Times, 21 November 1915, Section II, p. 20.

the use of credit in foreign trade. Many of them
insisted on immediate settlement of their bills instead
of granting the usual 90 day terms. Their reluctance
to discount their bills with a local bank represented
the carry-over of a domestic attitude toward the discount of promissory notes. That was mistaken, even
though understandable, and it reinforced the existing
bias in favor of cash dealings.

For their part, the banks were far from generous
in extending acceptance facilities even to prominent
foreign banks. They required a collateral deposit
before agreeing to accept endorsed notes. That practice
in effect violated the basis of true acceptance banking,
which was based on the proposition that a transaction
between reputable merchants or firms constituted an
asset in itself and therefore warranted the creation
of capital to finance it.[74] In addition, the banks
gave no indication through 1916 of developing a discount market that would assure bankers that they could
dispose of their acceptance holdings in return for
immediate cash. The flow of bills to England for discount had declined to a trickle from its postwar volume,
but that indicated only two things: first, that Federal

---

[74]Fred I. Kent Papers, Princeton University
Library, Box 1 Miscellaneous letters. Kent to J. F.
Schmid (Bankers' Trust) 12 October 1914.

Reserve Bank purchases and rediscounts of acceptances
provided an adequate substitute for a discount market;
and second, that with increased reserves the banks found
it more profitable to carry bills than to discount them
in London under existing rates.[75] American bankers
strove to overcome those obstacles to the sound development of foreign banking. Wartime confusion, and the
earnest sentiments of the leading bankers led them to
improvization in their efforts to assist the Allies.
While this helped to generate an immense increase in
the use of the dollar acceptance credit, it hampered
efforts to make the gain permanent.

---

[75]NYFRB, Strong Diary, 16 March 1916, record of
conversation with Sir Christopher Nugent of the Union
Discount Company of London.

Chapter III

Shaping Wartime Acceptance
and Discount Strategy

American bankers happily acknowledged the temporary international supremacy of American trade and
finance during the war, and regarded their primary
problem as being the one of maintaining as much of their
gains as possible. They generally agreed that the
preservation and development of American gold reserves
constituted the basic requirement for achieving that
goal. Paul Warburg, vice-governor of the Federal Reserve Board, argued in 1914 that, because Europe's
holdings of American stocks and bonds represented a
great potential drain on American gold reserves, the
Federal Reserve Board must construct a policy on discount rates that would provide credit facilities where
legitimate needs existed; but also maintained that the
rates had to be high enough to reduce the demand on
Federal Reserve Banks and at the same time discourage
too large a return of securities to the United States.[1]
It was a complicated problem, but the gradual accumulation of gold would create an increasingly large base

_____

[1]Federal Reserve Board Memo, n.d. /1914/, Warburg
Collection, Yale University.

for credit and invaluably aid the development of a world-
wide dollar acceptance system. That, in turn, would
provide a comfortable credit cushion against the end of
the war, when, as Warburg felt, relatively low American
long term rates would cause Europeans to cash their
American stocks for gold.

The reduction of minimum reserves by the Federal
Reserve Act and the enormous influx of gold generated
by increasingly favorable trade balances in 1915 and
1916 facilitated export expansion at relatively low rates
of interest. The New York Federal Reserve Bank assisted
the process by keeping its rates for banker's acceptances low even when rates on other short term paper
began to rise in 1916. A comparison of the discount
rates in New York and London for prime 90 day bills
disclosed a difference in favor of New York of 3 to $3\frac{1}{4}$%
per annum. In addition to this interest saving, the
difference in the initial cost of commission for the
issuance of the draft in dollars compared to a draft
in sterling amounted to another $\frac{1}{2}$% per annum.[2] The
favorable rate inevitably attracted American traders and,
facilitated by the number of bills of exchange drawn in

_____

[2]Alexander D. Noyes, The War Period of American
Finance (New York: 1926), p. 146. Ernest E. Ling
(manager of the Foreign Trade Department of the NCB)
Speech to the International Trade Conference of the
NAM, Proceedings, (NAM, 1915), p. 265.

dollars and accepted by American banks and trust companies, export commission houses and industrial concerns began to grow.

Even under these conditions however, the development of the close commercial ties between seller, the accepting bank, and the buyer, upon which a permanent system of American international finance depended, did not proceed at anything approaching the rate by which foreign trade expanded. Wartime conditions encouraged American manufacturers to ask for what amounted to cash terms of foreign buyers.[3] More important, the immediate needs of the Allied belligerent countries did not allow for the development of balanced trade, and the policies of the Wilson Administration forbade the use of long term paper to pay for exports. These factors, together with the single-minded determination of the New York financial community, led by J. P. Morgan, Benjamin Strong, Frank Vanderlip and James Brown, to support the Allies put abnormal strain on American short term credit and hindered the sound development of an American acceptance system.

While virtually everyone acknowledged at the outset the important role American credit would play in the

---

[3]Federal Record Center, Arlington, Virginia, RG39, Box 101, memo by William Woodard, George F. Peabody, and Benjamin Strong, 2 August 1915. Also Hamlin Diary, 30 December 1916, Library of Congress.

war, and in the related reinvigoration of the American
economy, President Wilson retarded the full expansion
of financial aid by asking for neutral behavior from
American citizens. Consequently the first American
exchange assistance to a belligerent (Morgan to the
French Government) required the transfer of French gold
to the vaults of Morgan, Harjes Company (Paris) in
return for a credit of $10 million on Morgan in New
York. A few weeks later, when the French approached
Morgan for an extension and an actual loan on credit of
$50 million, Secretary of State William J. Bryan said
that the government could not countenance such advances
to belligerents. Morgan obediently terminated the
negotiations. Within a few weeks, however, the Wilson
Administration clarified the State Department's position
so as to allow banks to grant credits to facilitate
foreign commercial transactions. But it maintained the
ban on the sale of foreign investments in the United
States.[4] The National City Bank immediately issued a
$10 million credit to the French Government, taking
French Treasury notes for security. In the ensuing

---

[4]New York Times, 30 October 1914, p. 1, Charles
Hamlin to McAdoo, 17 August 1915, Box 142, McAdoo Collection., L. C. Bryan indicated in a letter to Senator
Stone, 25 January 1915, that credit transactions for
the purchase of war supplies, where the money remained
in the United States, were not against the spirit of
neutrality. Ibid. This was also Wilson's view.

months, American banks issued a number of similar short
term loans to belligerent nations, including Germany.[5]

These credits tied up the resources of the banks,
however, and in an effort to free themselves from this
burden and yet remain within the ban on loan flotations,
several leading financiers resolved to tap the resources
of the Federal Reserve System through the discount
mechanism. The French appeal for additional credit
early in the summer of 1915 provided a test case for a
New York syndicate led by James Brown and including
Morgan and Company, the First National Bank, and the
National City Bank. Brown offered a group of French
bankers $20 million credit in the form of three-month
drafts, renewable three times for a total of 360 days.[6]
Theoretically, the syndicate banks would accept the
drafts, introduce them into the open market for discount
and, perhaps, eventual rediscount by a Federal Reserve
Bank. The French would have their goods, the banks

---

[5]From the beginning of the war to the end of 1915,
the U. S. advanced $902 million to belligerents
including Canada. Germany got $10 million. Annual
Report of the Federal Reserve Board, 1915 (Washington,
1915), p. 190.

[6]FRC Arlington, RG39, Box 101, Warburg to Strong,
11 June 1915. When the point of renewal credits had
been raised a few weeks earlier in connection with a
Russian credit, the Board decided that bills arising
from such credits could not be discounted. New York
Times, 25 August 1915, p. 2

would hold the notes for liquidation after a short term
and draw a handsome commission. The French government
agreed to secure the credit with Treasury notes and
provided that no moratorium would affect the obligation
of the French banks to pay the American acceptors.[7]
Clearly, the American syndicate had constructed the
terms of the credit to get around the requirements of
the Federal Reserve Act forbidding national banks from
accepting drafts running more than six months and Federal Reserve Banks from rediscounting acceptances
having more than 90 days maturity. The renewal feature
subverted the self-liquidating character of the customary 90 day bill, and the arrangement and conduct of the
business between a few banks on either side of the
water precluded the development of close commercial
connections between exporters and importers.

In spite of the obvious shortcomings of the plan,
the financial community of New York, completely disposed
to the Allied cause and, in view of the State Department's
ambivalent position on loans, quite willing to abandon a
specious definition of neutrality, took it upon itself
to win support for the Brown plan from the Federal
Reserve Board. In the face of the opinions of the
State Department, and the Board's own counsel, the

_____

[7]Hamlin Diary, Volume 3, 20 July 1915, Library of
Congress.

initial objections of some members of the Board to
extending the credits (because they involved contraband
cotton, munitions, boots and other articles of war)
quickly faded. International law held that all exports
were legal, and Secretary McAdoo assured Strong that
the government would "interpose no objection to the
facilitation of our export trade by making credit
arrangements in this country. There has not been on the
part of this government any objection to the opening of
credits or making of loans to foreign governments for
purposes of assisting in payment for commodities
purchased here."[8] The question remained, however,
whether or not Federal Reserve member banks could discount the renewal acceptances.

The Board of Governors revealed its intention to
preserve the spirit of the law (if not the letter) by
insisting that no member bank could enter into a contract that obligated it to accept a new draft against
the same transaction. The Board would make no legal
objection, however, if a bank wanted to make an independent arrangement to renew.[9] That procedure would

---

[8]FRC Arlington, RG39, Box 101, Franklin D. Locke
to Strong 29 July 1915. Hamlin Diary, Volume 3, 16 July
1915, Library of Congress. Draft of unsigned letter
/McAdoo/ attached to a letter from Strong to McAdoo,
2 September 1915, Box 143, McAdoo Collection, Library
of Congress.

[9]FRC Arlington, RG39, Box 101, Hamlin to Strong
28 July, 1915.

make the credits subject to fluctuations in the interest rate and permit responsive changes in terms. McAdoo
objected. He was alarmed lest the failure of the Board
to do everything possible to facilitate such credit (and
similar operations) should critically reduce American
trade. He wrote Charles Hamlin, Governor of the Board:
"It seems to me that the Board is going far afield
when it undertakes to control the discretion of the
officers and directors of a bank, as to whether or not
credit should be given, or refused either by extension
or otherwise, as long as the officers and directors
are acting within the law. Our duty is to protect the
commerce of the United States. Our foreign commerce
is just as essential to our prosperity as our domestic
commerce. In fact, they are so intimately related that
one depends upon the other. To my mind there can be
no differentiation between them."[10]

The bankers, attempting to outflank the Board by
enlarging the context of the dispute, invited McAdoo
to meet with directors of the New York Federal Reserve
Bank. They explained that their war financial strategy
was not dissimilar from Warburg's except in regarding
the sound development of an acceptance system. Given
the existing stage of the war, they argued, the United

[10]FRB 332.215, McAdoo to Hamlin, 7 August 1915.

States as the greatest producing nation was having its
export balance of trade affected favorably while its
import trade declined sharply because of the blockades
and the needs of the belligerents. "From that time
until the conclusion of the war, the problem," as they
saw it, was "to keep our export commerce going, as its
continuance and its extent will depend very largely upon
our willingness to extend credit."

The major problem, they emphasized, was to find a
means of extending credit to foreign customers so that
"our shipments of cotton, grain, and other kinds of
exports" did not suffer curtailment.[11] The solution
was for the financial community to induce American
exporters, along with English and continental exporters,
to use dollar credits. But that plan was blocked by
the reluctance of American merchants and manufacturers
to draw bills of exchange for exports when they could,
in the exigency of war, demand cash.[12] Moreover, the
directors pointed out, the banking machinery lacked
sufficient connections with world commerce and the
bankers themselves had little acquaintance with foreign
firms. Neither would they give acceptance credits

[11]FRC Arlington, RG39, Box 101, Memo by William
Woodard, George F. Peabody, and Benjamin Strong,
2 August 1915, subsequently submitted to McAdoo.

[12]Ibid.

except upon undoubted collateral.

"It is becoming daily more evident," they concluded, "that the 'commercial' credits necessary for the security and continuance of our export trade must, to some extent, be represented by bills drawn by foreign banks on American banks and discounted in our market."[13] Anticipating a reversal of the American exchange position after the war, when "we may experience a flood of foreign manufactured goods for sale in our markets," and "our manufacturers will face the severest competition that they have ever experienced,"[14] the New York bankers further supported the creation of dollar acceptances and the accumulation of such bills for which reimbursement could be later required from foreign markets when demand on American gold began. On the basis of these observations, they recommended the further liberalization of regulations of the Federal Reserve Board to permit foreign firms and institutions to draw bills payable and discountable in the American market, and similar changes to allow the accumulation of gold reserves in Federal Reserve banks.[15]

---

[13]Ibid.

[14]Ibid.

[15]Ibid.

Impressed by this thesis, both Secretary McAdoo
and Secretary of State Robert Lansing (on McAdoo's
urging) warned President Wilson that the United States
must liberalize its loans for its own welfare. Otherwise, Lansing argued, "the result would be restriction
of outputs, industrial depression, idle capital and idle
labor, numerous failures, financial demoralization, and
general unrest and suffering among the laboring
classes."[16] Though he favored breaking relations with
Germany, Lansing remained sensitive to the President's
design for neutrality. Yet even he could invent no
way of rationalizing freer loans with American neutrality and, after mature deliberation, could only
recommend that the nation pursue its own self-interest
and disregard the appearance of neutrality.[17]

Paul Warburg, whose resistance to this line of
thought and close ties to Germany made him vulnerable
to unfounded charges of pro-Germanism, thought such a
policy would weaken the foreign expansion of American
banks.[18] He wrote Strong that if the United States

---

[16]NARS, RG59, 811.51/2624a, Robert Lansing to
Woodrow Wilson, 6 September 1915.

[17]NARS, RG59, Lansing to Wilson Letterpress,
24 August 1915. NARS, RG59, 811.51/2624a, Lansing to
Wilson, 6 September 1915.

[18]FRC Arlington, RG39, Box 101, Warburg to
Strong, 8 September 1915.

discouraged finance drafts, as he termed the renewal
credits, it would be in a position to force Europe to
turn over its regular acceptance business for the financing of commercial transactions. American banks could
then gradually create the necessary branches and direct
contacts.[19] Warburg admitted that, before such connections were made, the banks might have to arrange
such transactions for the account of foreign banks;
but argued that they would at least be based on self-
liquidating commercial transactions and not, as under
the Brown credit proposal, mere financial arrangements
divorced from the commercial world.[20]

On McAdoo's insistence, however, the Federal
Reserve Board ruled that a national bank could enter
into an agreement for a revolving credit extending more
than six months. "It is not the province of the Board,"
it explained, "to deal with problems involving international relationships of the United States either for
the purpose of restricting or extending exportations."
The Board, however, believed "that the financing of the
country's export trade is at the present time one of
the most important financial problems with which the
nation has to deal; and it is of the opinion that the

---

[19]Ibid.

[20]Ibid.

Federal Reserve banks cannot, even if they would, avoid their legitimate and proper share of responsibility in this process of financing."[21]

The New York financial community quickly exploited its policy victory. The syndicate swung into action with more than 10 New York banks accepting drafts. Unleashed by the Board's ruling, The New York Federal Reserve Bank began to purchase the acceptances on the open market, or to rediscount them when offered by the syndicate banks. The credits tied up the banks' operating capital in acceptance bills and increased money rates, but the New York Federal Reserve Bank kept the bankers acceptance rediscount rate low enough to give the renewal paper a favored position.[22] Strong also bought for the account of other Federal Reserve Banks, and before long the Boston, Philadelphia, Cleveland, Chicago, and San Francisco banks became heavy holders of the renewal credits.[23]

---

[21]Annual Report of the Federal Reserve Board, 1915 (Washington, 1916), p. 9. The Board and the press looked upon the move as a means of developing an American discount market. New York Times, 11 September 1915, p. 4 and Ibid., 25 August 1915, p. 2.

[22]FRC Arlington, RG39, Box 101, James Brown to Strong, 1 December 1916. Federal Reserve Bulletin, 1 November 1916, p. 590-591. Regular banks could not compete with the New York Federal Bank's 2% rate. At the time, the London bank rate was 5%.

[23]Annual Report of the Federal Reserve Board, 1916 (Washington, 1917), passim.

It soon became apparent that the renewal acceptances were not self-liquidating, however, and that the
debtors required new loans to pay off the old and
needed additional loans to continue the flow of goods.
Warburg wrote Strong with some irritation in June 1916
that Federal Reserve banks held a bit more than
$17 million in acceptances of the renewal type out of
a total holding of about $60 million in acceptances.[24]
"If we are planning to pay off these from the large
French loan transactions now under contemplation well
and good," he wrote; but "if not and these drafts are
to be renewed from time to time since they are not self-
liquidating, we ought to set some limit up to which we
are willing to buy this class of paper."[25] Even Strong

[24]FRC Arlington, RG39, Box 101, Warburg to Strong,
21 June 1916. By November, the Federal Reserve System
held $30 million of a total of $80 million outstanding
French renewal credits. See Munitions Hearings, 1936,
Volume 8, p. 9956, Warburg to Strong 10 November 1916.
Earlier in the year, Harding had sent Strong a long,
firm memo on the need for limiting the amount of syndicate acceptances and advocating direct contact between
individual banks and borrowers. Harding to Strong and
memo, 7 February 191 6 in Munitions Hearings, Volume 8,
p. 9953, "Instead of forming syndicates guaranteeing
the interest rate to the acceptor," he wrote, "banks
should make agreements with manufacturing concerns to
buy acceptances." Ibid., p. 9952.

[25]FRC Arlington, RG39, Box 101, Warburg to Strong,
21 June 1916. In addition to the French export credit
of 21 August 1915 for $20 million, the New York Federal
Reserve Bank was buying acceptances from a French
credit of 27 December 1915 of $15 million and another
of 10 March 1916 for $15 million. The French paid

admitted that the credits "were wrong in principle and
would not prove effective in correcting the exchanges
permanently."[26] As a result of conversations between
M. Pallain, Governor of the Bank of France, and the
Paris Chamber of Commerce, France sent a representative
to meet with the big New York bankers to promote the
opening of credits on that basis. This resulted in the
unique French Industrial credits of 1916 arranged by
the Guaranty Trust Company, the Bankers Trust Company,
and J. P. Morgan and Company. The deal involved between
165 American banks and 75 French firms, and included
mining, metal, automobile, construction, and petroleum
concerns.[27] In spite of this arrangement, however,
undifferentiated acceptance credits between the banks
of the respective nations continued to finance most of
the non-governmental trade transactions between America
and the Allied belligerents.

As it became clearer that the renewal credits were
not self-liquidating, Federal Reserve Board opinion
began to coalesce in support of Warburg's resistance

---

about 6 3/4% for the credits. See Munitions Hearings,
1936, Volume 8, p. 9987-9993. The French obtained a
$100 million credit shortly after this in October, 1916.

[26]FRC Arlington, RG39, Box 101, memo of 13 June
1916, Strong.

[27]Munitions Hearings, 1936, Volume 8, pp. 10027-
10040.

to the credits. Another $100 million French renewal
credit in October of 1916 caused the new Governor of
the Federal Reserve Board, W. P. G. Harding, to raise
the issue with Secretary McAdoo. "It seems to me that
this transaction comes pretty close to financing for
the French government, and if the Board, in view of the
very general publicity that is being given the proposed
credit, takes no notice of the statements that these
acceptances... which you will note can be renewed for
a period of 18 months, are available for rediscount at
Federal Reserve banks, it would put itself by its
silence, in the attitude of sanctioning such statements."[28]
Perhaps more seriously, Harding pointed out that if the
Federal Reserve banks were obliged to hold the renewal
credits in increasing amounts, then the possible
absorption of so large a part of bank reserves might
have a marked effect on money rates affecting the farm-
ing and stock raising interests and domestic trade
generally.[29] Moreover, the renewal credit arrangements
weakened the effectiveness of the entire System in regu-
lating money and gold flow because the French credits,
once extended, could not be discouraged by increasing

---

[28]FRC Arlington, RG39, Box 101, Warburg to Strong,
23 October 1916. FRB 205.001, W. P. G. Harding to
McAdoo, 21 October 1916.

[29]Ibid.

the Federal Reserve rediscount rate. Such increases
would merely hit the American banks who would be obliged
to go on making the renewals to France at the usual
rate.[30]

The Board's resistance came at the very time when
the Wilson Administration was striving for a negotiated
settlement of the war. Harding expressed the fears of
many when he wrote Strong that American credit policy
reminded him of railroad finance: "...if the company
went broke the whole community, including the bank,
would be broke. I cannot escape the conclusion that
the United States has it in its power to shorten or
prolong the war by the attitude it assumes as a banker
.... if we sell on a cash basis our foreign trade will
be confined to more reasonable limits and will fall off
gradually, as the ability of foreign nations to pay
diminishes."[31] Strong had ambivalent views on the
issue. They pivoted around his single-minded devotion
to see the Allies win the war. He chose to bend with
the current of opinion for the moment and admitted to
Harding that the war ought to be stopped and thought
Wilson could accomplish that task.[32] Out of a desire

---

[30]FRC Arlington, RG39, Box 101, Warburg to Strong,
23 October 1916.

[31]Ibid., W. P. G. Harding to Strong, 16 November 1916.

[32]Ibid., Strong to Harding, 20 November 1916.

for harmony with the Board, he even hinted that he might
approve a differential interest rate for the renewal
credits that Warburg had proposed.

He made it clear, however, that he considered
peace and the renewal credits secondary to securing the
nation's gold in Federal Reserve Bank vaults, putting
them in a position to redeem in gold every dollar of
paper money in circulation by enabling them to get
together "a thousand million dollars or thereabouts"
in excess of their required reserves.[33] With that
amount of gold in hand, Strong had little fear for the
nation's financial security and, although he did not
make this explicit, the arrangement would permit the
greatest possible extension of credit to the Allies.
He wrote Warburg that Wilson could do "little if anything" to end the war, and in that context re-emphasized
the need to secure the nation's gold reserve.[34]
Adequate protection lay "in having all Europe in pawn,"
rather than in any program that interfered with "the
operation of natural laws and those which have been
accepted between nations as lawful and proper."[35]

------

[33]Ibid.

[34]FRC Arlington, RG39, Box 101, Strong to Warburg,
28 November 1916. Strong did not believe that the
United States could build a real acceptance business
under wartime conditions.

[35]Ibid.

The Board blocked the renewal credit in a circular
sent to Federal Reserve agents on October 23, 1916.
"Banking prudence and obligations to the commercial
interests of the country," it announced, "require that
Federal Reserve Banks should be conservative in
acquiring these acceptances." Strong, the New York
syndicate, and the press opposed the decision, arguing
that unless the United States granted the foreign
credits freely the country ran the risk, not of terminating the war, but (by accepting only gold for payment)
of causing an inflation of prices and credits.[36] The
Board maintained its position, strengthened by the
unanimous support of the influential Federal Advisory
Council which included prominent bankers from every
reserve district. The Advisory Board expressed the
fear that if the war continued for a long period, even
the strongest nations would be in a critical financial
position, and that would force those making short term
loans to take long term bonds, a step the bankers considered inadvisable.[37]

---

[36]FRC Arlington, RG39, Box 101, Warburg to Strong,
23 November 1916.

[37]Ibid., Warburg to R. H. Treman (Deputy Governor
of the New York Federal Reserve Bank), 23 November
1916. Even Strong's friend and confidant, James Brown,
the original sponsor of the renewal credits became
"disturbed about the lack of a real, open, market for
acceptances." The italics are Brown's. Nor did

In this context, Henry P. Davison, partner in the
J. P. Morgan Company (purchasing agent for Great
Britain and France) visited the Board in Washington to
announce the intention of his firm to float a $100
million dollar issue of British bonds. Davison argued
that Morgan & Company only wanted to do what was best
for the country. The British government was buying
nearly $10 million of goods a day, and if it could not
get loans the Board would have to take the responsibility
for the cut in the nation's trade.[38] Governor Harding
repeated to Davison the warning he had given Strong.
There was some danger of becoming so involved with one
debtor that the United States would be drawn deeper and
deeper into the conflict. When the rest of the Board
expressed the feeling that "we had grown enough and that
we should be in a position of contemplating the 'breaking out' of peace without a thought of alarm," Davison
asserted that he proposed to issue notes as fast as the
market would take them in quantities he supposed would
reach $500 million to $1,000 million.[39]

Strong's explanations meet Brown's questions as to why
such a market had not been encouraged by the Federal
Reserve Bank. See Munitions Hearings, Volume 8,
p. 9970, Brown to Strong, 1 December 1916.

[38]FRC Arlington, RG39, Box 101, Warburg to Strong,
23 November 1916.

[39]Ibid., and Federic A. Delano to Strong, 19 December 1916.

President Wilson secretly strengthened the Board's
hand by suggesting to it that its position had not been
firm enough and could be made still more positive.
The Board issued a second pronouncement advising bankers
to proceed with "much caution" in sinking their funds
in long-term obligations, or in investments that were
short-term in name but which, either through contract
or force of circumstance, might have to be renewed
until normal conditions returned. While this meant
that "abnormally stimulated export trade to some countries" would decline, the backflow of American
securities in payment for goods would sustain the
economy and, moreover, "trade can be stimulated in
other directions."[40]

The announcement hit the market so hard that Davison was not only unable to float the notes, but was
forced to buy nearly $20 million in exchange outright
to continue his purchases for Great Britain. "We cannot maintain this pace even for a few days," a partner
told Jack Morgan.[41] The Bank's warning panicked the

---

[40]Hamlin Diary, Volume 4, 27 November 1916, L. C.
Federal Reserve Bulletin, 1 December 1916, p. 661-662.
Europeans tended to hold on to their American investments, considering them the safest form of investment
for their money during the war. New York Times,
29 March 1915, p. 8 and Ibid., 8 June 1915, p. 16.

[41]Hamlin Diary, Volume 5, 13 January 1916. Also
Munitions Hearings, Volume 8, p. 8557, Lamont to
Morgan, 28 November 1916.

financial community and stopped other and more desirable
forms of international finance. Harding hastened to
emphasize to the financial community that the pro-
scription concerned renewal credit alone. "The board
merely sought to call attention to the fact that as
this country had become an important market for foreign
securities," he explained to the Boston City Club, "the
same businesslike habits which are well established
regarding domestic loans should be developed in marketing foreign flotations."[42] The French Ambassador, at
first very bitter about the warning as an attack on
French credit, later acknowledged that Davison had badly
bungled the whole matter. The British Ambassador,
Cecil Spring-Rice, concurred. Both men felt that
Davison had forced the Board to take a stronger stand
than it might otherwise have done.[43] A prominent member of the Bank of England expressed wonder that the
United States had not acted long before to check the
free and easy credit policy, "and if it had done so...
it would have benefited not only the United States but
also perhaps, indirectly, /England/ by forcing us to

---

[42]FRC Arlington, RG 39, Box 101, James Brown to
Strong, 1 December 1916. New York Times, 15 December
1916, p. 17.

[43]Hamlin Diary, Volume 5, 13 January 1917 and
Volume 4, 30 December 1916.

become more self-supporting.[44]

In the months that followed, exports dropped and
the financial community attributed this to the Great
Britain's new policy of economy arising from a lack of
ease in financing. Sir Edward Holden remarked with
some asperity that the United States had acquired a
good deal of the Allies' gold and hence "it seems difficult to understand why the Federal Reserve Board
should have endeavored to place difficulties in the
way of American bankers creating further loans."[45]
Finally, under criticism from home and abroad for its
"conservative" policy, the Board felt obliged to rein-
terpret its warning, positively recommending that the
favorable balance of trade be financed out of savings
but still proscribing the renewal credits.[46] The banking community expressed itself well pleased with the
new statement. They felt it clarified misunderstanding
and had the effect of smoothing the way for further
foreign issues. Within a month, however, the United
States entered the war against the Central Powers, the
New York Stock Exchange was closed to the flotation of

---

[44]Brien Cocayne to Strong, 15 January 1917, FRC
Arlington, RG39, Box 101. Cocayne, Deputy Governor
of the Bank of England, became Governor in 1918.

[45]New York Times, 27 January 1917, p. 1.

[46]Ibid., 9 March 1917, p. 11.

foreign securities, and the American people, sub-
scribing unprecedented amounts for Government bonds,
financed the heavy loans which the Allies required for
the continued purchase of war supplies in America.

Without question, the Treasury Department dominated
the Board of Governors of the Federal Reserve System
before the United States entered the war in April 1917.
After that, the Treasury controlled all fiscal operations of the country by placing American international
finance on a government-to-government basis. Since
payments for American goods came directly out of American loans, the proportion of dollar exchange used to
finance American trade increased rapidly, and by far the
greater part of the commodities which at the time the
United States entered the war were being paid for by
drafts in foreign currencies came to be paid for directly by the Allied governments out of American loans.[47]
Acceptances increased dramatically, although the
market for them remained for the most part in the
purchases of Federal Reserve banks. The New York
Federal Reserve Bank, which alone purchased $112,664,681
in 1916, bought acceptances worth $387,550,190 in 1917

---

[47]Albert Rathbone, "Making War Loans to the
Allies," reprinted from Foreign Affairs, April 1925
in Munitions Hearings, 1936, Volume 8, p. 9207.

and doubled that figure in 1918.[48] The bankers themselves began to modify the habit of discounting their
own acceptances in response to a heavy barrage of
propaganda from the System. That action contributed
to the development of an open market. Several groups
of New York bankers had begun by 1918 to handle the
function of discount banks, and for that purpose developed a broad discount market to replace their dependence
on Federal Reserve Banks.[49]

---

[48]Annual Report of the Federal Reserve Board,
1917 (Washington, 1918), passim. Ibid., 1918. In
1918, New York and Massachusetts allowed savings banks
to purchase acceptances. New York Times, 6 May 1918,
p. 15. For an example of the propaganda circulated
among bankers to persuade them to use acceptances see
Srinivas R. Wagel, "The Importance of Acceptances in
Making the United States a World Financial Power," in
the Journal of the American Bankers' Association,
March 1917, p. 717.

[49]Federal Reserve Bulletin, August, 1918, p. 695.
New York Times, 10 October 1918, p. 15. Federal
Reserve Bulletin, October 1918, p. 930. Annual Report
of the Federal Reserve Board, 1918, p. 60. New York
Times, 12 April 1918, p. 17. By the end of 1918, four
discount companies existed, all in New York: The Union
Discount Company developed especially to handle cotton
bills; The Discount Corporation of New York, directed
by the officers of the major New York banks including
J. P. Morgan, James Stillman, Charles Sabin (of
Guaranty Trust); The Foreign Trade Banking Corporation
managed by the former exchange wizard of the Guaranty
Trust, Max May; and the First National Corporation,
owned by the First National Bank of Boston, mainly
engaged in handling the new business developing in
Latin America and the Far East. The First National Bank
of Boston had established a branch in Buenos Aires in
1917. For evidence of reform of the bankers' habits see
Annual Report of the Federal Reserve Board, 1917,
p. 261-268, and p. 220.

Before United States entry into the war, the Board
formalized the arrangement that Strong had made with
the Bank of England in 1914 that enabled the Bank of
England and the Federal Reserve Bank of New York to
maintain deposit accounts and represent each other in
the purchase of bills of exchange for the purposes of
stabilization and to reduce the necessity for expensive
international shipments of gold.[50] The arrangement,
common among European central banks but a milestone in
American banking growth, allowed the New York bank,
acting for the entire system, to accumulate exchange
at favorable rates and buy bills against dollars "on
unusually favorable terms." Warburg favored the plan,
a tribute to the way he controlled his personal and
business ties with Germany. The arrangement was so
advantageous in Strong's view that he suspected that,
had there been no war, Warburg would have "viewed the
arrangement with exaltation."[51] In the months following,

---

[50]FRC Arlington, RG39, Box 101, note dated
16 January 1917.

[51]FRB 301.2-6, J. H. Case, Deputy Governor, New
York Federal Reserve Bank, to W. P. G. Harding,
27 August 1918. The respective shares of the Federal
Reserve Banks in the accounts opened at the New York
Bank were as follows: Boston, 7%; New York, 34.5%;
Philadelphia, 7%; Cleveland, 9%; Richmond, 3.5%;
Atlanta, 3%; Chicago, 14%; St. Louis, 4%; Minneapolis,
4%; Kansas City, 5%; Dallas, 3.5%; San Francisco, 5.5%.
They contributed in proportion to the amount of their
capital to the funds the New York bank used for
foreign exchange purposes. Forgan had been one of the

the New York Federal Reserve Bank made correspondent
arrangements with the central banks of most of the
Allied powers.[52]

The United States Treasury agreed to cooperate with
England in counteracting wartime pressure on sterling
by buying it in unlimited quantities at a fixed rate.
This meant that sterling bills from all over the world
flowed to New York for redemption.[53] The administration had little choice but to provide the support.
The collapse of sterling would have wrecked international trade and Americans lacked sufficient overseas
banking development to reconstruct the system. While

---

suggestors of the plan. See FRB 301.2, Forgan reply to
FRB questionnaire, 20 February 1917. Banks outside of
New York did not share in the large balances of the
loans kept on deposit in New York banks by Allied
nations. The Treasury maintained that it could make no
suggestion to the governments all of whom had been
transacting heavy business before United States entry
into the war and had consequently established banking
connections before the United States government had
extended any loans. See NARS, RG56, Box 55, Russell C.
Leffingwell (Assistant Secretary of Treasury) to J. B.
Forgan (chairman of the Chicago Clearing House)
15 October 1918.

[52]FRC Arlington, RG39, Box 101, Strong to Frederic
A. Delano, 22 September 1916. The State Department had
held up the arrangement until after the American presi-
dential election of 1916 recognizing in it a threat to
America's neutrality position. Ibid., Strong to
R. H. Treman, 31 August 1916.

[53]Albert Rathbone, op. cit., in Munitions Hearings,
Volume 8, p. 9207-9212. Also, Noyes, War Period of
American Finance, p. 227.

the banking community readily admitted that a failure
to support sterling would be too costly, it made known
its desire for a compensatory reduction in the amount
of sterling and an increase in the amount of dollars
used in international transactions.[54] Governor Harding
wrote Secretary McAdoo that he wanted to force the
American dollar into the position of being a standard
currency for the world and to require those nations
who have to deal with the United States to do so in
dollars.[55] After the United States entered the war,
the Treasury's arrangements generally carried out
Harding's wish that the British make American purchases
in dollar acceptances on American banks liquidated by
subscriptions to Liberty Loans placed to the account
of England.

London nevertheless generated more than twice the
volume of bills as New York. Moreover, London was
beginning as early as 1918 to recapture some of the
foreign trade business it had temporarily lost to the

_____

[54]Munitions Hearings, Volume 8, p. 9373-9374,
Harding to McAdoo, 14 August 1917. Also FRB 421.2-7,
Archibald Kains (president, American Foreign Banking
Corporation) to McAdoo, 28 August 1917. Kains wrote:
"...this would be an opportune time to make the London
bankers relinquish to some extent, in our favor, their
hold on the world's commerce."

[55]Munitions Hearings, Volume 8, p. 9373,
Harding to McAdoo, 14 August 1917.

United States. The New York Federal Reserve Bank had
begun to raise its rates in 1916, partly to encourage
the formation of an open market for acceptances and
partly from pressure on its reserves. While the
English rate fell from 5% to about 3 7/8% the New York
rate climbed steadily to a level between 4% and
4 1/2%.[56] This meant that American merchants found it
profitable to draw on London banks as they had done
before the war.

The Board's regulations, as they had evolved by
1918, permitted bankers to use acceptance credits in
producing, manufacturing, acquiring, or carrying goods
both at home and abroad, in all cases where there was
a bona fide contract to export or import from the
United States (or between any two countries) within a
reasonable and specified time.[57] For example, New
York bankers participated in financing Cuban sugar
planters between crops, and in the grinding and carrying

---

[56]Annual Report Federal Reserve Board, 1918, p. 19
and Federal Reserve Board 332.21-17, Warburg memo,
7 January 1918. Some experienced American exporters
had expected the London rate to drop below New York's
and had never abandoned their British connections.
Hough, Practical Exporter, p. 460.

[57]FRB 332.21(2), Memo regarding financing foreign
productions of commodities by bankers acceptances
credits, E. R. Kenzel (Investment Manager of the New
York Federal Reserve Bank) to Pierre Jay (Federal
Reserve Agent, New York), 6 November 1918, p. 4.

of sugar in Cuba. However, much of this sort of business
in staple crops that was clamoring for credit turned
to British and Canadian banks. They were eager to do
the business and were prepared, after sterling rates
declined, to offer rates competitive with New York.[58]

The New York Bank's investment expert, protesting
an adverse Board ruling, claimed that the United States
had not developed its export trade in any line where
there had been foreign competition, because of "our
inability or unwillingness to grant credit."[59] Broadly
speaking, however, the Board made every effort to
improve the American competitive position in trade
finance and even considered (ultimately to reject)
raising the limit of acceptances to 200 per cent of
each bank's capital and surplus.[60] At first ruling on
technical grounds against the eligibility of certain
drafts drawn against the International Products Company (an important American venture in canning and

---

[58]Ibid., and Hearings Before the Committee on Bank-
ing and Currency on the Federal Reserve Foreign Bank
(Washington, 1918), p. 108, United States Senate, 65th
Congress, 2nd Session.

[59]FRB 332.21(2), Kenzel Memo.

[60]Annual Report, Federal Reserve Board, 1918,
p. 868. Strong claimed that one of the largest New
York banks had increased its surplus by $5 million in
order that their line might not be exhausted. FRB
332.21-17, Strong to Warburg, 18 January 1918.

exporting South American meat) the Board reconsidered
its decision. After a few alterations in wording, it
ruled the firm's drafts eligible for discount at Federal
Reserve Banks.[61]

To encourage the banks to expand their foreign
connections, the Board successfully asked Congress in
1917 for an amendment allowing Federal Reserve Banks
to open and maintain accounts in foreign countries.
This would have put the Reserve banks in competition
with their member banks. The New York Reserve Bank did
not favor the amendment. New York banks with foreign
operations were opposed to competition from central
banking establishments, especially their own.[62] Though
the amendment passed, the Reserve banks did not act
upon it.

Senator Robert L. Owen of Oklahoma, a sponsor of
the Federal Reserve Act who had fought for government
control of the system, sought to take this arbitrary
control of acceptances and foreign exchange out of the
hands of the New York banks and give exporters "easier
access to the banking credits of the United States."[63]

[61]FRB 332.215, W. P. G. Harding to New York
Federal Reserve Bank, 19 November 1918.

[62]Hamlin Diary, Volume 4, 18 December 1918. These
conflicts involved the Bank of Japan and the Bank of
the Philippines.

[63]Federal Reserve Foreign Bank Hearings, p. 107.

The heavy outflow of dollar exchange resulting from
American purchases and support of sterling exchange
had produced a dollar surplus in Spain, Italy, Argentina and several other countries with which the United
States enjoyed no compensatory trade. The result was
a severe discounting of the dollar in those nations.
The New York Federal Reserve Bank could not easily cope
with the problem, and Owen seized upon the weakness as
an additional reason for advocating a specially created
Federal Reserve Foreign Bank to keep exchange at par
abroad.[64] The entire banking community (including the
Federal Reserve Board) opposed Owen's bill, just as
they had fought McAdoo's similar idea in 1914. This
time the Secretary of Treasury joined the bankers.
The bankers argued that the foreign exchange market
demanded hard scrabbling, and that any further extension of Federal banks into the field would deprive them
of their legitimate business. The Federal Reserve
Board and the Treasury Department saw their interests
threatened by Owen's bill because both of them
desired a free hand in controlling foreign exchange;
the former during the war period and the latter after
the war.[65] They agreed that the only remedy for the

---

[64]Ibid.

[65]FRB 301.2-9, /Harding7 to Strong, 7 September
1918. NARS, RG56, Box 55, Warburg to Russell C.

exchange problem involved restricting imports and
increasing exports to those countries. Secretary
McAdoo assured President Wilson (who had expressed
strong interest in Owen's plan) that the War Department, the War Trade Board, and the War Industries
Board had already begun to give proper direction to the
export business.[66] This virtually unanimous opposition
killed Owen's bill.

As the war came to a close, the American foreign
banking system had progressed far along the lines
envisioned for it by Paul M. Warburg, Frank Vanderlip,
and other designers of the system. The Federal Reserve Board had enlarged the versatility of an American
acceptance system and had increased its use as an
instrument of trade among American bankers and merchants. The New York Federal Reserve Bank, dominating
the discount and foreign exchange markets, provided a
stability to the nation's international finance similar

Leffingwell, 11 October 1918. Ibid., Strong to Harding,
6 September 1918. H. P. Meserve to Vanderlip,
29 August 1918, Vanderlip Collection.

[66]FRC Arlington, RG39, Box 96, Strong to Leffing-
well, 7 August 1918. Ibid., Box 95, McAdoo to Woodrow
Wilson, 26 September 1918. FRB 301.2-9, Strong to
Warburg, 20 June 1918. Vanderlip to Russell C.
Leffingwell, 21 September 1918, Vanderlip Collection.
About the only big banker favoring Owen's plan was
Max May of the Foreign Trade Banking Corporation.
See Federal Reserve Foreign Bank Hearings, p. 61.

to what had been sought by the proponents of the
Aldrich or "bankers" bill of 1912 through a central
bank. The New York bank maintained close connections
with some of the most powerful central banks in the
world and, in addition, several member banks had begun
to form a respectable network of branch banks abroad
and discount houses at home which challenged the British
system in the postwar world.

Yet the American system had not generated acceptance in numbers comparable to the British system.
While the acceptance liabilities of the Guaranty Trust
Company surpassed those of the largest London acceptance house, authorities estimated liabilities of all
New York banks at $210 million in 1918; whereas those
of London banks were $500 million.[67] Before the war,
London generated $1 billion annually in acceptances.
Even more significantly, the financial world doubted
the permanence of the American phenomenon. The heavy
reliance of bankers on the New York Federal Reserve
Bank meant that New York lacked a real discount market
that would facilitate investment in acceptances and
make them readily negotiable and therefore popular credit
instruments.

---

[67]Estimate of Leopold Frederick (director American
Smelting and Refining Company, Treasurer of the Braden
Copper Company, and the Chile Copper Company) in The
London Economist, 21 December 1918, p. 831.

Perhaps an even greater obstacle to the supremacy
of the American system lay in the comparative unfamil-
iarity of American bankers and manufacturers with
traditional practices of international finance. The
biggest bankers and the government had exercised too
much power from the top. They had arranged international credits while the ordinary businessman remained
ignorant of the practices of financing world trade.
The National City Bank viewed postwar prospects with
alarm because even "well-informed business leaders do
not seem to appreciate the present American facilities
for giving adequate banking service to all sound export
business that can possibly arise."[68] Psychologically,
American business was not fully prepared for the
American export thrust that was expected to follow the
war.

---

[68]From The Americas, National City Bank's publication, quoted in The New York Times, 22 December 1918,
p. 19.

Chapter IV

Expanding and Protecting Long-Term Commitments

The war focused the attention of American bankers
on the significant shift in America's position in the
international economy. European investments in the
profitable American market had shown a steady increase
prior to 1914, rising by about $200 million a year.
American investments abroad fluctuated from year to
year, but they seldom exceeded the inflow of foreign
capital. During the war, however, that pattern was
reversed and the United States loaned more, sometimes
much more, than it borrowed.[1] The close connection
between the wartime increase in the export of American
goods and the simultaneous rise in American capital
exports led many bankers and government officials to
advocate a neo-mercantilist form of government protection of American investments abroad in order to
maintain the American export trade.

The United States had a chequered, though not
unimpressive, record as a foreign investor before the
war. Direct investments, mostly in extractive industries

---

[1]Historical Statistics of the United States, United
States Bureau of the Census, Washington, D. C., 1960,
p. 564.

in the Western Hemisphere, constituted about 75 per cent
of a total foreign investment of $3.5 billion. In
addition, American financiers had loaned to Mexico,
Japan, Germany, Cuba, Santo Domingo, Argentina, China,
Liberia, and Austria. From the standpoint of foreign
capitalists, American portfolio holdings were less
impressive than the total indicated because the American investor's commitment of funds was usually
temporary, and he relied on the ready convertibility
to dollars of his portfolio holdings at the major
European stock exchanges.[2]

The accumulated foreign holdings of American stocks
and bonds ran into billions of dollars. In June 1914,
the total exceeded $7.2 billion. As American exports
rose during the war, massive sales of foreign-held
American securities helped pay for those goods. By
the end of 1915, the United States had absorbed about
$1.5 billion of its own securities.[3] They were

---

[2]Mortimer Schiff, Remarks, Proceedings of the
International Trade Conference, National Association
of Manufacturers (New York, 1915), p. 303. The National
City Bank felt obliged to conduct its international
loans on joint account with banks in London, Paris,
and Berlin in order to secure an international market
for such loans. Milton V. Ales to Secretary of State
Philander Knox, 7 April 1909, memo of conversation with
Knox on 5 April 1909. Vanderlip Papers.

[3]New York Times, 18 December 1915, p. 18.

liquidated in such amounts, particularly by England, as to threaten the stability of the stock market. Through the influence of Secretary of the Treasury McAdoo and the New York financial community, J. P. Morgan arranged the first large long-term assistance to the belligerent powers. It was designed, in part, to protect the market by reducing the need for England and France to sell American holdings in exchange for war materials.[4] Under those arrangements, the repatriation of American securities took place, for the most part, in a rising market until mid-1916.[5] At that time, Morgan arranged another large loan for the express purpose of retarding the sale of British stock in New York.[6]

In addition to repatriating those obligations, American bankers and investors loaned enormous sums to the belligerent nations, which had been creditors of the

---

[4]New York Times, 27 February 1915, p. 15. Ibid., 5 July 1915, p. 10. This was a debatable point. Benjamin Strong argued that large loans or credits had to be made to reduce the premium in dollar exchange. Strong to McAdoo, 2 September 1915, NYFRB file of Strong Correspondence 1914-1919. See Chapter III. Shortly after the Wilson administration agreed to the principle of renewal credits, English Treasury officers negotiated the first long-term loans with New York bankers.

[5]New York Times, 10 August 1916, p. 12.

[6]Ibid., 25 February 1916, p. 14 and 13 August 1916, p. 2.

United States. Before American entry into the war, those loans were as follows: Great Britain, $1,131,400,000; France, $736,700,000; Russia, $148,500,000; Italy, $25,000,000; and Germany, $10,000,000.[7] The corollary of this European dependence upon capital importation was the cessation of European capital exports to Latin America, China, and other debtor nations.[8] The possibility of establishing close commercial relations with those countries by providing them with American loans excited the interest of financial circles in New York and, in turn, prompted a debate over the proper policies for the banks and the government to pursue in stimulating investment abroad.

No clear cut policy emerged from the discussion, and American investment in those areas did not increase significantly. But the debate revealed the goals (and dilemmas) of the banking community and the government during a period of sharp transition. A review of Wilson's policies toward China, Mexico, and Latin America reveals the drift of the debate, and its effect on the foreign economic policies of his administration.

[7]Economic World, 31 March 1917, p. 437-439.

[8]NARS, RG42, Box XXV, L. S. Rowe (Treasury Department) to W. G. McAdoo, 5 October 1915.

The Taft administration had encouraged the most
powerful New York investment banks to enter an international consortium with British, French, and German
bankers to finance the development of Chinese railroads,
mines and public utilities. The administration's
objective was to prevent the division of China into
spheres of influence and to promote an open door for
future American trade expansion.[9] The American members, National City, Morgan, Kuhn, Loeb and the First
National Bank (all investment banks of the first class),
hoped to profit from the financial transactions involved
in developing China through the consortium. Negotiations over several proposed projects broke down,
however, and the Chinese Revolution of 1911 channeled
the consortium's activities in other directions:
particularly toward reorganizing the finances of the
Chinese government.

The new goals of the consortium did not seem immediately profitable to the Americans but they acquiesced
in the policy decisions of the more powerful European
bankers in deference to the State Department's desire
to preserve the open door. In its final form, the
consortium's policy resulted in the addition of Russian
and Japanese bankers to the original group and the

[9]Herbert Croly, <u>Willard Straight</u>.(New York: Mac-
Millan Company, 1925), p. 37.

recognition of their special spheres of influence in Manchuria, eastern Mongolia, Mongolia, and western China. In short, the consortium in operation was functioning against the open door policy.[10] The bankers and the State Department reconciled themselves to the situation with the thought that the new consortium would restrain the other powers from seizing upon the opportunities arising from the Revolution to extend their economic interests at each others expense.

The terms of the proposed loan gave the consortium controls over the expenditure of the funds and over the collection of revenues promised as security by the Chinese.[11] For this reason, the new Chinese government, fired by the nationalistic spirit of the revolution, never agreed to the consortium proposal. The Americans in the group, who anticipated little profit from such operations as the consortium now contemplated, expressed their desire to leave.[12] Only

---

[10]Martin J. Sklar, "Woodrow Wilson, The Six-Power Consortium and Dollar Diplomacy," (unpublished masters' thesis at the University of Wisconsin, 1962), p. 125.

[11]Ibid., p. 129.

[12]Ibid., p. 159. Frank Vanderlip to James Stillman, Vanderlip Mss., Columbia University Library, 4 February 1909, also 21 March 1913. Willard Straight, Journal of Race Development, "Chinese Loan Negotiations," Volume 3, p. 408.

the pleas of the Taft administration deferred this
decision until March 1913.

The incoming Wilson administration confronted the
issue during its first weeks in office. The bankers
expressed their intention to withdraw unless Wilson
would specifically request them to carry on and offer
them some assurance of a speedy conclusion of the loan
negotiations. The consortium was already discredited
as an instrument for promoting American operations in
China, and Wilson could not give such assurances as the
bankers demanded. He disliked the monopoly features
of the consortium arrangement which blocked the operations of independent American financial interests.
Moreover, the strong influence over Chinese affairs
sought by the consortium bankers disturbed Wilson.[13]
In amplifying his reasons for refusing the bankers'
request, Wilson explained that the United States could
not promise support "because it did not approve of the
conditions of the loan or the implications of responsibility on its own part which it was plainly told by the
bankers would be involved in the request." The
responsibility "might conceivably go to the length in
some unhappy contingency of forceable interference in

_____

[13]Ibid., p. 164-165.

the financial, and even political, affairs" of China.[14]
The bankers eagerly withdrew.

Wilson's position did not mean, however, that he
had abandoned the government's commitment to American
foreign financial expansion. On the contrary, the
President clearly understood the importance of the
Federal Reserve System in this regard and specifically
promised the bankers to use it as an alternative technique to the consortium.[15] Moreover, the Wilson
administration did not refuse to support independent
American financial efforts in China which did not
involve interference in official Chinese financial or
administrative affairs. Even in the months immediately
following the American withdrawal from the consortium,
when the Chinese government sought a loan from American
financial sources, the Wilson administration "fully
endorsed the proposed loan" and promised "all proper
diplomatic support."[16]

Nevertheless, misunderstanding of Wilson's consortium statement clouded the meaning of his foreign
financial policy. Businessmen incorrectly concluded
that he had abandoned the open door and would not support

---

[14]Ibid., p. 165.

[15]Willard Straight, Journal of Race Development,
Volume 3, p. 408.

[16]Ibid., p. 174.

Americans in getting their fair share of the world's business. The bankers also feared that Wilson, in limiting the administration's commitment to measures less than extreme, had seriously hurt their efforts to build confidence for the sale of what they believed would be a growing volume of foreign paper on the American market.[17] This feeling persisted even beyond the formation of the Second Chinese Consortium under Wilson's auspices in 1917.

The Investment Bankers Association of America took steps to protect and promote their broadening interest in foreign investment. At the Third Annual Convention of the Association in 1914, John J. Arnold, vice-president of the large First National Bank of Chicago, sounded the first note of what was to become an important theme of the Association. "The American investment banker of the future," he said, "must acquaint himself with world conditions."[18] A foreign relations committee was formed and assigned the task of establishing a "foreign information center" to provide American investors, on a subscription basis, with information on investment prospects in foreign lands. But the committee, composed of representatives of fairly influential

---

[17]Ibid., p. 229.

[18]Proceedings of the Third Annual Convention of the Investment Bankers Association of America, 1914, p. 69.

investment houses, displayed small interest in the
project. From the start, the foreign relations committee saw its real task as the formation of a
protective association to represent the interests of
American foreign investors to the American government.[19]

At the 1916 convention, the chairman of the foreign
relations committee reported that there was little
reason to continue the committee unless its function
was changed from information to protection. Other
members extolled the values of the Foreign Bondholders
Corporation of London. "So great is the moral influence of the Council of Foreign Bondholders," said one
committee member, "that only after it effected a
satisfactory settlement with defaulting governments
could any material amount of money be raised in
Great Britain by such governments."[20] The committee
reported to the 1917 convention its conclusion that it
ought to be reorganized as a new committee that would
develop a scope and power similar to that of the London
Foreign Bondholders Committee. That task would mean
keeping in touch with the authorities at Washington
and "by...mobilizing the investment resources of the

---

[19]Ibid., 1916, Report of Barrett Wendel, Jr.,
chairman of the foreign relations committee, p. 37.

[20]Ibid.

country the influence exerted would be tremendous!"[21]
Not much later, the executive officer of the Investment Bankers' dissolved the small foreign relations
committee and replaced it with a new and powerful
foreign securities committee. It was composed of representatives from the most important banking and
investment houses in the country and, headed by
Thomas W. Lamont (J. P. Morgan), it took charge of
defining the Association's post-war orientation to the
world.[22]

The outbreak of the war provoked a drive for
expanded shipping and banking relations with South
America, and that led to an anxious increase in cooperation between the Wilson administration and the
business community. The necessity of providing
American replacements for British trade and investments in South America, and the opportunity for
permanently ending the American dependence on British
banking facilities, dominated the expressions of the

---

[21]Ibid., 1917, p. 139.

[22]Ibid., 1918, p. 193. The Committee did not
develop as intended and, in 1924, reported against the
advisability of organizing a permanent institution
similar to the British Corporation of Foreign Bondholders. Instead they recommended continuing the
existing policy of forming a protective committee for
each particular national problem, e.g. Mexico, Russia.
George W. Edwards, Investing in Foreign Securities
(New York: The Ronald Press, 1926), p. 296.

public press and commercial journals. Almost simul-
taneously came the realization that the United States
could not develop the desired connections--even during
the war--without increasing imports from South America
and extending long-term investments that would provide
South American nations with the funds to buy American
goods.[23] Men experienced in international finance
warned that even more would be necessary to maintain
the South American connections. Charles M. Muchnic,
vice-president of the American Locomotive Sales Corporation, spoke for more than one American financier when
he said that American bankers and the investing public
"must realize that only through American investments
in and control of great enterprises in South and
Central American countries can we hope to get our share
of the trade with these countries."[24] Existing British
investments in Latin America of $4 billion were the
natural target of this policy, though the $2 billion
held by French and German interests was also important.[25]

------

[23]New York Times, 26 November 1915.

[24]Ibid., and New York Times, 4 October 1915, p. 4.
Annual Convention of the National Foreign Trade Council,
1917, p. 374 and 382.

[25]For the figures see William Lough, Banking Opportunities in South America, U.S.G.P.O. Washington, D. C.,
1915, p. 20. Also see New York Times, 28 January 1916,
p. 8 for remarks of James Farrell of U. S. Steel.
Also, New York Times, 4 October 1915, p. 4.

As a result, widespread approval welcomed the creation of the American International Corporation, a foreign investment company organized by the nation's most powerful manufacturing, transport, and financial interests to promote foreign trade. The National City Bank and the Guaranty Trust Corporation, the leading banking members of the Corporation, anticipated profits from marketing the investments and from financing the expected trade. The members subscribed $50 million and planned to finance public works, private undertakings, and municipal loans. They expected to take securities as collateral from the borrower.[26]

Frank Vanderlip, head of the National City Bank, reported the Wilson administration as being "really very pleased" with the AIC, and described a luncheon of the directors of the Corporation with the Secretary of Commerce as "a lovefeast." Misunderstandings between Washington and the business community over Wilson's consortium policy appeared to have vanished and, to Vanderlip at least, the administration seemed "earnestly of a mind to cooperate."[27] The AIC first moved into Uruguay, loaning that government $4 million for a

---

[26]NARS, RG /signature illegible7 to Secretary of State Robert Lansing, 16 December 1915. 811.5034 Am 3/-.

[27]Frank Vanderlip to James Stillman, 7 January 1916, Vanderlip Mss., Columbia University.

sewerage and water system project. The AIC stood to
gain 25 per cent of the construction profit through
arrangements with its subsidiary engineering firm, in
addition to the commission for marketing the bonds.
The AIC had by 1916 created large interests in the United
Fruit Company, International Mercantile Marine Corporation, Pacific Mail and Steamship Company, Allied
Machinery Company, and was engaged in careful scrutiny
of Brazilian ore deposits, Central American railroads,
and a possible Chinese railway loan and contract.[28]

The firm developed a capital investment policy for
Latin America that excluded investments of less than
$500,000, and any loans to undeveloped private enter-
prise. "The time was not yet ripe to offer investors
at home securities for new enterprises so the issue is
secured by nothing but the concession."[29] The corporation sought the following type of investments: 1) the
construction of public works, taking payment in bonds
of the government involved; 2) long-term investment
for the further development of well-established enterprises; and 3) straight loans to federal, state, and
municipal governments. It planned to take the smallest

[28]Charles Stone (president of AIC) to Frank Vanderlip, 13 March 1916, Vanderlip Collection.

[29]NARS, RG59, 823.51/129, enclosure in letter of
Edw. T. Morgan to J. Butler Wright (State Department),
12 September 1916.

possible risk by taking its security in the form of governmental taxing powers or existing capital assets (which were largely the result of European risk and capital). The policy seemed realistic from the corporation's point of view because the war had denied South America its customary supplies of European capital. Even so, the corporation did little South American business. It first concentrated on its shipping interest, the United Fruit Company and, after American entry into the war, emphasized the construction and operation of the immense American ship building complex at Hog Island.[30]

American capital displayed little interest in filling the gap left by Europeans. Latin American countries obtained no more than $70 million from the United States during 1915 as compared to the annual $750 million taken from Europe in pre-war years.[31] By the time the United States entered the war, South Americans had floated loans in New York totalling no more than $160 million. These debts were for the most part contracted by the governments of Argentina, Uruguay, Bolivia and Panama. As Paul Warburg explained, the highly profitable European demand for American

---

[30]Charles Stone to Frank Vanderlip, 17 December 1919, Vanderlip Collection.

[31]International Trade Conference, 1915, p. 325.

goods captivated American manufacturers and bankers,
"and prevented them from going out into the world try-
ing to conquer new markets that would be of permanent
value."[32] The National City Bank's $15 million loan
to Argentina in 1915, though a dramatic event in the
American financial world, did not initiate an era of
American hegemony in Latin America. The City Bank
later refused Argentine requests for capital, and
granted credit only in the form of short-term bankers'
acceptances which it could rediscount at the Federal
Reserve Banks.[33]

Other American banks did make small loans to
Brazil and Uruguay in an effort to take advantage of
European financial embarrassment there. But those
operations did very little to encourage a feeling of
financial solidarity with the United States, and the
public press of both continents frequently carried confidential expressions by commercial men that, after the
war, the South American trade would return to its old
European centers because of the failure of American
traders to supply long-term capital. A Treasury officer

---

[32] Paul Warburg, speech at Buenos Aires, 3 May 1916
in The Federal Reserve System, Volume 2.

[33] /signature illegible7 to C. V. Rich of the
National City Bank, Vanderlip Collection. 22 March
1915. The Bank also turned down financing for
Brazil.

responsible for developing commercial and financial
ties with Latin America reported that "the people of
Chile and Peru are anxiously awaiting the termination
of the present conflict because it will enable them
again to turn to the European manufacturer for cour-
teous treatment and the continuance of the system of
credits."[34] The American business leaders and government officials who were concerned could only recommend
that industries with considerable trade at stake consider the necessity of protecting that trade by
obtaining for their customers some relief in the form
of investments. If judiciously made, those would yield
a fair return and meanwhile provide a market for
American material which could not otherwise be sold.

When the Wilson administration attempted to
encourage the bankers to take a more active role in
South America and elsewhere, they threw Wilson's dis-
couraging consortium policy back in his face. A
vice-president of the National City Bank publicly
lamented in 1915 the discontinuance of Knox's dollar
diplomacy, "...in actually putting someone through the
open door...because it meant taking issue with the

---

[34]NARS, RG42, Box XXV, L. S. Rowe (Treasury) to
W. G. McAdoo, 5 October 1915. Also see NARS, RG43,
minutes of the United States section of the Central
Executive Council of the International High Commission, 23 September 1915.

world on the Orient." "Ought there," he asked in the
same speech to the United States Chamber of Commerce
that had been organized with Taft's help in 1910, "be
any question that a citizen investing in the instru-
mentalities of trade in foreign lands, purchasing
property and securities and making contracts in the
furtherance of our commerce, or even in building up
good will for his particular goods and business in some
other part of the world, should not be promptly protected in his rights in case they should be threatened
through the failure of government, injustice, oppres-
sion of confiscation?" "Is there any hope," he warned,
"that this work abroad will be carried on, under
competitive conditions, unless there is a certainty of
such protection."[35]

Though extremely keen on expansion, especially in
South America, the Wilson administration was slow in
replying to this challenge. Secretary of Treasury
McAdoo sponsored the Pan American Financial Conference
in 1915 to promote financial connections between the
North and Southern halves of the hemisphere. European
interests were excluded. After a series of private
meetings and public speeches. McAdoo and the

---

[35]Samuel McRoberts, (vice-president National City
Bank) speech to United States Chamber of Commerce,
3 February 1915.

International High Commission (which emerged as the
executive body of Pan-American activities) concluded
that there was very little they could do to encourage
more capital to go to South America because of the
profitable European business. Their plans were "put off
because of the general disturbance."[36]

But McAdoo's determination died hard. Not long
after the conference, he began to press the State Department for assurances of protection for American
investors abroad. "We have such an extraordinary
opportunity in South America that we ought not to lose
it," he wrote, "merely from an unwillingness, on the
part of the Government, to give to our bankers and investors the same reasonable assurances that Great
Britain and other first class powers give to their
bankers and investors under similar circumstances.
I should think every step short of armed intervention
would be a reasonable step, and I think that would
probably satisfy... Unless we can do this we may as
well stop, in large measure, our efforts to do anything
in South America... I hope that your Department may be
able to determine upon a policy which will encourage

[36]NARS, RG43, Proceedings of the Central Executive
Committee of the International High Commission, United
States Section, 17 October 1918, Volume 1, p. 68.

our people to go ahead with the development of South America."[37]

Lansing replied quickly but uncertainly. "I feel, as you do," he wrote, "that the Government should protect American bankers and investors; but the question is - how far the Government is warranted in pledging its support in advance. The President had indicated in his statement of March 1913, re: China, the limit to which the administration would go in this respect, and the State Department, of course, is bound by the position then taken unless the President desires to draw a distinction between China and the South American republics.... Assuming that the cause is deserving, the extent to which the Government should go in backing up Americans might, I think, be covered by your phrase - 'every reasonable step' - which of course leaves it open to the Government to decide what, in the circumstances of each particular case, is reasonable. The Government has in the past supported its representations by breaking off all diplomatic relations, by a show of force, and by the use of physical force. On this point, I think we are not far apart...I have not formulated definitely views in this matter and, of

_____

[37]NARS, RG59, 835.51/160, McAdoo to Lansing, 23 August 1915.

course, will not do so without consultation with the President."[38]

American policy in the case of the Mexican revolution illustrates how far the administration could go in protecting American business interests while at the same time exhibiting, as in the Chinese consortium episode, a reluctance to intervene forcibly in the financial and political affairs of another nation. It is true, of course, that Wilson earned the enmity of some American oil and financial interests for his opposition to the dictatorial government of General Victoriano Huerta. American oil and financial interests felt Huerta was a man they could do business with, and Wilson obstinately blocked any rapprochement on the grounds of his dislike for Huerta's bloody political tactics. But Wilson's policy of "watchful waiting" <u>and working</u> for Huerta's downfall was part of a very strong program for the restoration and protection of American property rights in Mexico.[39]

The intentions of the new Carranza Government to control Mexican oil reserves with the cooperation of

---

[38]Lansing to McAdoo, 30 August 1915, McAdoo Papers, Library of Congress, Box 143.

[39]This is clear from Samuel Flagg Bemis, <u>A Diplomatic History of the United States</u> (New York: Henry Holt and Company, 1942), p. 548. Also see Robert F. Smith, The Formation and Development of the International Bankers Committee on Mexico, <u>Journal of Economic History</u>, December 1963, p. 575.

foreign oil companies did not prevent its *de facto* recognition by the Wilson administration in 1915. Later, word that Carranza was preparing a decree for the nationalization of the petroleum industry drew warnings from the United States State Department and steps to block nationalization.[40] The pressures included the 15,000 American troops sent into Mexico in July 1916, to put down the border raids of the renegade Pancho Villa. Wilson allowed his representatives to make it clear that the withdrawal of the troops was contingent upon the acceptance by the Mexican Government of the proposals of the Mexican-American High Commission then negotiating the restoration of relations between the two governments. The most important proposals of the American Commissioners included the protection of the property of foreigners and their right to resume operations of properties owned before the Revolution.[41] That would preclude nationalization of the oil industry.

The Mexican Commissioners regarded the withdrawal of the American troops as a non-negotiable issue, and they refused to discuss the status of foreign claims until the United States took that action. During that

---

[40]Robert F. Smith, unpublished manuscript on American-Mexican Relations, p. 17.

[41]Ibid., p. 18.

confrontation, the Mexican Constitutional Convention was
in session, and the possibility that the nationalization
of resources would become part of Mexican fundamental
law alarmed the American Commissioners. To prevent
this, they advocated the withdrawal of American troops
so that the State Department would send an ambassador
to negotiate directly with Carranza before it was too
late.[42] Wilson withdrew the troops but consistently
worked for the protection and restoration of American
property in Mexico. During World War I and post-war
period his principal openings resulted from Mexico's
desire for recognition by the United States and for
loans. For this reason the International Bankers Committee on Mexico assumes some importance as an instrument
of American foreign policy.

The Committee represented a combination of international financiers to which the Mexicans would almost
certainly have to appeal for assistance. These interests exercised their influence on behalf of the holders
of securities of the Mexican Republic, The Mexican
Railway System, "and generally of such other enterprises
as have their field of action in Mexico."[43] The State
Department approved this arrangement under the

---

[42]Ibid., p. 12.

[43]Edgar B. Turlington, Mexico and Her Foreign Creditors (New York: Columbia University Press, 1930), p. 277.

conditions that "the policy of the United States Government regarding Mexico be the dominating influence in
the operations of the group."[44]   In deference to the
"special position of the United States in relation to
Mexico," the Committee yielded to American members "a
predominant position in all questions of major policy
in spite of the fact that Britain and France held by far
the greater financial interest.[45]

The Bankers' Committee entered into negotiations
with Mexican representatives for a loan in February
1919. The terms included a Treaty of Amity and Commerce which would provide "a satisfactory basis for the
operation of business enterprises in Mexico by the
nationals of other countries." Carranza rejected the
proposal. When Carranza's Government fell in 1920, the
State Department further strengthened its Mexican
policy by withholding recognition until the new government signed a treaty with specific guarantees for
foreign property rights.[46] To increase the pressure,
loans were to be postponed until after recognition.
The Mexican Government resisted the pressure and, instead

[44]Smith, "International Bankers Committee,"
p. 580-581.

[45]Turlington, p. 276.

[46]Smith, "International Bankers Committee," p. 584.

of capitulating to the formal American demands, expressed its friendly intentions towards American
property interests. The State Department remained
adamant. French and British members of the International Committee, impressed by the growing stability
of Mexico, pushed the Committee towards private
negotiations with the new government. The State Department reluctantly yielded but Wilson blocked the move
because he did not want any discussion of loans prior
to recognition. The President felt such action would
only make Mexico less conciliatory.[47]

The later development of Wilson's Chinese policy
also reflected his great willingness to provide more
support for American business and finance abroad. After
the withdrawal of the American group from the consortium,
the Chinese extended tempting offers to independent
American financial interests with the enthusiastic
support of the American minister Paul Reinsch. The
State Department began informal negotiations with the
members of the American group in 1915-1916 to revive
their interest in China.[48] The bankers were not
optimistic. The European members of the consortium,

[47]Ibid., p. 585.

[48]Frank Polk, Memo as Office of the Counselor to
the State Department, 26 July 1916, Polk Papers, Yale
University.

because of a shortage of capital, would not be able to participate, but the American bankers felt that commitments to their European partners prevented them from doing business independently.

Other American interests were meanwhile actively investigating possibilities for investment in China. One of them, the Commercial and Continental Trust Company of Chicago, concluded arrangements in December 1916 to lend $5 million to the Chinese. When asked by the bank for a statement of policy regarding the transaction, the State Department replied encouragingly: "The State Department is always gratified to see the Republic of China receive financial assistance from the citizens of the United States. It is the policy of the department now as in the past to give all proper support and protection to the legitimate enterprises abroad of American citizens."[49] American banking and Asian interest took this to be a modification of the policy laid down by Wilson over the consortium in 1913.[50] European and Japanese interests, which had accustomed themselves to the view that American capitalists were not going to take a prominent part in the

[49]Asia, December 1916, p. 324, "American Capital in China."

[50]Ibid., and Frank Vanderlip to Jeremiah Jenks, 4 August 1916, Vanderlip Mss. In addition, the Wilson administration dispatched a Commerce Bureau man to the

development of China, were somewhat startled. The
British and French began making offers of cooperation
with the Americans. The Japanese, who had made over-
tures for a cooperative partnership in China with the
United States furnishing the capital while the Japanese
handled the management, began to have second thoughts
about working with the Americans.[51]

The State Department had not, however, drastically
changed its position on the consortium. Early in 1917,
in a conversation with the Japanese ambassador over the
possibility of reviving it, Secretary of State Lansing
repeated the administration's view that "such cooperation... appeared to be a political combination
interfering with China's sovereign rights." He believed
that international cooperation in China was a good
thing, but insisted that it should be kept free from
political motives.[52] President Wilson approved
Lansing's stand: "I think the position you took was
the right one throughout the conversation," he stated.
Lansing again reaffirmed Wilson's 1913 position in the

Far East to study investment possibilities there. New
York Times, 13 April 1917, p. 15.

[51]NARS, RG 893.51/1731, Ambassador to China Paul
Reinsch to Lansing, 9 December 1916.

[52]NARS, RG59, 893.51/1743, Secretary of State
Lansing's memo of a conversation with the Japanese
Ambassador, 25 January 1917.

summer of 1917 in an interview with the Belgian
ambassador. Lansing stated that the Wilson administration had opposed the consortium because they felt
there should be competition for loans in China "and
because concerted action by the powers appeared to
involve political control to an extent in China."[53]
But the pressure for change was apparent in Lansing's
personal observation. "My own view that the whole
question, being of so much importance to our future
relations in the Far East, ought to be considered with
little regard to the past."[54]

Financial developments in 1918 did force a recon-
sideration of the administration's consortium policy
along the lines suggested by Lansing. In the summer
of 1918, the Continental and Commercial Trust Company
declined to exercise the option to loan again to the
Chinese. Rumors began to fly that Japan would make the
loan and secure it with the Chinese wine and tobacco
tax. The American Tobacco Company complained to the
State Department that such a loan would give the Japanese control over the Chinese tobacco market, and warned
that this would ruin American interests worth $30 million

---

[53]Ibid.

[54]NARS, RG59, Lansing to Woodrow Wilson Letterpress, 25 June 1917.

a year.[55] According to J. B. Duke of the company, the
Japanese would extend these methods to other commodities
and gradually exclude American exports of all kinds
from China. Duke's complaint was the immediate basis
of a State Department conference which led directly to
the formation of a new consortium with the full support
of the Wilson administration.[56] The bankers said that
the only approach they would consider involved either
the advance of the money to the government of China by
the government of the United States, or the advance of
the money to the government of China by private bankers
with the cooperation of the United States government.
"Our investors must be satisfied of the willingness of
our government to make, in conjunction with other governments, prompt, vigorous, and strong representations
to be followed by such other action as might be
necessary to secure a carrying out of a foreign contract
made in good faith."[57]

---

[55]NARS, RG59, 893.51/1906-1927. These dispatches
cover the general background. J. B. Duke made out his
case in 893.51/1905, 18 June 1918 to the Secretary of
State.

[56]J. B. Duke to State Department, 18 June 1918,
NARS, RG59, 893.51/1905, 1906.

[57]Undated, unsigned and untitled memo in the
Breckenridge Long Papers, Box 180. Long was the major
negotiator between the State Department and the New
York bankers. The same phrase appears in a draft of
the bankers' letter to the State Department in the files
of the War Trade Board, RG182, Box 58. Also NARS,

The State Department agreed to consider the proposition with the idea of making an expression to the bankers "which should, as far as government policies would permit, encourage them in the project." The exact terms that the government offered the bankers are not clear, but a State Department officer observed in July 1918 that the New York bankers were "delighted" with the State Department understanding of the plan, an understanding communicated to them with the approval of President Wilson.[58] The plan was consummated in the same month, and Willard Straight, one of the organizers of the original consortium which had been dashed by Wilson in 1913, was wholly satisfied. "It is exactly the basis on which I worked with the State Department in the days of the old American group."[59] The consortium had been re-established at the request of the Wilson administration, and was more than ever an instrument of national policy in the Far East.

RG59, 893.51/1916½, Memo of a meeting, 26 June 1918, between J. P. Morgan, Jacob Schiff, Frank Vanderlip, Russell Leffingwell (Assistant Secretary of Treasury) and Albert Strauss)(Treasury Department). Breckenridge Long, then Third Assistant Secretary of State was also present.

[58]Breckenridge Long, Desk Diary, entry for 4 and 5 July 1918, Breckenridge Long Papers, Library of Congress.

[59]Willard Straight to Edward N. Hurley, 31 July 1918, Edward N. Hurley Papers, personal letters file 1581-1610, Notre Dame University Library.

The Chinese, however, remained as definitely hostile to
the new consortium as they had been to the old one, and
it lapsed into 'inactivity'.[60]

From any perspective, the Wilson years show a
strong movement by both government and private finance
into the world arena. Wilson's enthusiasm for the
Pan-American Financial Conference of 1915, the cordial
reception shown the formation of the American International Corporation, the concern for the development
of a supportive Latin American policy, the Mexican
policy, and the re-creation of the Chinese consortium
all illustrated the administration's interest in the
construction of a protective umbrella over American
foreign interests.

The irony of Wilson's foreign financial policy is
that it impressed the public mind, especially before
1920, as weak and excessively restrained. Even those
who should have appreciated Wilson and the State
Department's efforts expressed their concern. Thus,
Mortimer Schiff of Kuhn, Loeb, charged Wilson with
failure to protect the rights of American investors in
Mexico "not even to the extent of seeing that customs
duties specifically pledged to bondholders have been

---

[60]James G. Angell, Financial Foreign Policy of the
United States,(New York: Russel and Russell, 1965),
p. 88.

made available to them."[61]   Charles Evans Hughes' remarks
during the campaign of 1916 can be put down to political
motives, but those post-election remarks of William
H. Taft must carry greater weight.   Taft told the Rubber
Association of America early in 1917 that "if it was to
be understood abroad that this country would never resort
to extreme measures to protect American citizens of
corporations in foreign lands against the unlawful
invasion of lawless foreign Governments" then American
foreign enterprise would be fatally injured.[62]   The
audience interpreted the former President's remarks as
referring "to present conditions in Mexico" as well as
to contingencies which might arise in other foreign
countries.

As late as 1919, Fred I. Kent of the Bankers
Trust Company, touring Europe, found "that the Mexican
policy of the United States is a great drawback to
healthy reconstruction, because it has placed a great
fear in the minds of foreign interests as to our
attitude toward anarchy."[63]   Even the perceptive

---

[61]Remarks of Mortimer Schiff, NAM, International
Trade Conference, 1915, p. 307.

[62]New York Times, 9 January 1917, p. 3.

[63]Kent to Seward Prosser (Guaranty Trust Company),
28 August 1919, Box 1 miscellaneous letters, Kent
Papers, Princeton University Library.

Assistant Secretary of the Treasury Russell C. Leffingwell could write Wilson in 1919 that most Americans
had the feeling "that our historic policy is one of
indifference to the protection of American life,
property, and investments abroad."[64] With the Mexican
policy almost certainly in mind Leffingwell felt, like
Kent, that Wilson's approach could prove one of the
greatest obstacles to reconstruction.

All Wilson's efforts to protect American property
rights abroad and to extend the sphere of American
foreign operations could not permanently reassure the
financial community. This was partly a problem in
communication. So long as the government maintained
the option of not acting in a specific situation, business interests did not have confidence in protection.
Then again, the drawn-out Mexican episode (utilizing
manipulation and restrained force) had alienated
American business interests from its Mexican properties
for years. Business groups were never convinced that
prompt, forceful action would not have settled that
situation satisfactorily.

Finally, the bankers in the post-war world found
themselves facing great international responsibilities

---

[64]Russell C. Leffingwell to Woodrow Wilson, 22 July
1919, FRC, Arlington, Virginia, World War I Records,
Box 105, European Reconstruction folder, 1918-1919.

that were intensified by the broken condition of the important European economies. The need for strong government support seemed more important than ever. That estimate motivated the bankers (joined by major business interests) to urge the government to undertake distinctly new responsibilities in foreign relations: financial responsibilities in addition to traditional diplomatic protection. As Leffingwell warned the President, "Before the war ours was a debtor nation, now it has become a creditor of most of the world. A change so fundamental may well justify, even necessitate, a change of policy."[65]

---

[65]Ibid.

Chapter V

Reconstruction and Its Responsibilities

The American economy in 1918 exported goods valued
at about $6 billion. Exports of manufactured goods had
increased by 400 per cent, and agricultural goods
climbed 300 per cent over 1915. Imports had dwindled
to $3 billion, and the favorable balance of trade in
goods and services had increased to nearly $2.5 billion.[1]
That level of trade required government loans and a tremendous increase in the use of the bankers' acceptance
in dealing with the belligerent allies. When acceptance liabilities reached $284,737,000 in January 1918, a

---

[1] Historical Statistics of the United States,
Colonial Times to 1957, Washington, D. C., 1960, p. 544.
As a result of the war, American merchants and manufacturers, along with bankers, attached greater
importance to foreign operations and made greater commitments in that activity. Manufacturers secured the
Webb-Pomerene Act in 1916, which freed them from some
of the restrictions of the Sherman Act by allowing them
to combine to meet foreign trade competition. By the
end of 1918, 80 export organizations, each representing
united manufacturers in such areas as steel, copper,
textiles, and sugar had notified the Federal Trade
Commission of their intention to operate under the
provisions of the act. An increased willingness to
use bankers' acceptances and to finance their own
foreign business when money was not readily forthcoming
from banks paralleled the growing interest in foreign
trade shown by the formation of the Webb-Pomerene
organizations. New York Times, 16 March 1919, p. 19.

total near the legal limit, the bankers pressured the
Federal Reserve Board to raise the ceiling.[2] They won
that battle and, finding good profits in the acceptance
business, they sought to extend the practice. More
importantly, they also tried to protect their youthful
system of financing trade from the intense postwar
competition they expected.

Financial pressure had driven the open market rate
for bankers' acceptances in New York to $4\frac{1}{4}$% by the
middle of 1918. Even at that rate, however, bill brokers
found banks preferred to put their money in the call
loan market for the stock exchange at 5 and 6%.[3] This
reduced the liquidity of the bills, threatened to raise
their cost and reduce their utility. London with an
open market rate of about $3\frac{1}{2}$% was soliciting business
in New York, and sterling exchange competed favorably
with American acceptance dollar exchange in foreign
markets. To stave off collapse, the American acceptance system required a source of funds willing to
forego the high profits of the call loan money market.

---

[2]New York Federal Reserve Bank Records (NYFRB), File
440, Strong to Warburg, 18 January 1918. At this time
the Federal Reserve Board limited the acceptances of most
member banks to 100 per cent of their capital and surplus.

[3]NYFRB, 440, R. M. O'Hara (Deputy Governor) to
B. G. McCloud (Cashier, Federal Reserve Bank of Chicago), 30 August 1918. NYFRB, 790, Russell C. Leffingwell (Assistant Secretary Treasury) to Benjamin Strong,
4 February 1918.

The New York Federal Reserve Bank stepped into the breach and began buying bills at 4¼%, but only on the condition that the bill dealers repurchase the bills within 15 days. Shortly thereafter, Morgan and Company and the Guaranty Trust Company (and subsequently other banks) shouldered the responsibility for the system by making loans on call to discount houses and dealers against eligible acceptances at 4½%. This stimulated the market for acceptances and increased the purchases of the bills, albeit slowly. Banks continued to look upon the acceptance more as a new method of finance rather than as a short-term investment. The call loan market remained a strong competitor for short-term funds. Consequently, bankers tended to give little attention on increasing their portfolios of bills relative to the amount of acceptances they made.[4] Moreover, the call loan market continued to offer more attractive interest rates to short-term investors.

The financial strength of the United States, and the undoubted opportunities offered by the postwar world, encouraged American banks in making other commitments to foreign trade. To build an extensive

---

[4]NYFRB, 440, O'Hara to McCloud, 30 August 1918. See also New York Times, 24 August 1918, p. 10. New York Times, 27 August 1918, p. 13. FRB /?7 Sharp (International Banking Company), 18 July 1919. John Rovensky (vice-president National Bank of Commerce of New York), "The Acceptance as the Basis of the American Discount Market," New York, July, 1919 (pamphlet).

acceptance financing system, and to relieve the Federal
Reserve Banks of the burden of supporting it, the
bankers' American Acceptance Council launched a drive
to encourage the use of foreign and domestic acceptances, and to organize more acceptance and discount
houses. Bankers had established two large discount
companies in New York, and one each in St. Louis and
Chicago, by June 1919.[5] In New York, banks led by the
Guaranty Trust Company formed the Foreign Trade Corporation whose sole purpose was to accept bills of
exchange. The corporation could do business safely at
the level of 10 times its capital; i.e., $50 million a
year. Several banks in the mid-west opened foreign
trade departments to provide short-term credit, to
accept and discount bills of exchange, and to supply
foreign credit information.

The demand for American dollars in Europe led to
the establishment of a number of American banks in Italy,
France, and Eastern Europe. Two American banks entered
the French colonial empire by organizing, with the
Comptoir National D'Escompte, the French-American Banking Corporation with capital of $2 million and surplus
of $500,000. The National Bank of Commerce of New York

[5]New York Times, 6 April 1918, p. 19. Commercial
and Financial Chronicle, 24 January 1920, p. 332. New
York Times, 1 March 1919, p. 17.

and the First National Bank of Boston planned to share
in this way in accepting and discounting the short-term
paper of French colonial trade. The Comptoir maintained
200 branches throughout the world and had close connections with French colonial banks in Algeria, Egypt,
East Africa, Madagascar, Martinique, and Indo-China.[6]
The National City Bank continued its branch bank development by sending an organizing officer to establish
Paris headquarters at the beginning of 1919. The Bank
penetrated the financial terra incognita of Eastern
Europe with the formation of the People's Industrial
Trading Corporation to finance some of the immediate
postwar needs of Poland. Through the International
Banking Corporation, the City Bank opened a branch at
Lyon to finance the Far East silk trade to that indus-
trial city. And in 1919 it opened 35 branches to raise
its total to 50 throughout the world.[7]

The American Foreign Banking Corporation, established in 1917, expanded further in South America and
the Caribbean, and received permission from the Federal
Reserve Board to increase the ratio of its acceptances

[6] New York Times, 30 April 1919, p. 15. Commercial
and Financial Chronicle, 3 May 1919, p. 1765. Ibid.,
10 May 1919, p. 1874.

[7] Commercial and Financial Chronicle, 31 January
1920, p. 434. Frank Vanderlip to Bureau of Citizenship,
State Department, 23 December 1918, Vanderlip Collection.

to its capital and surplus from 6:1 to 12:1, which
increased its capacity to approximately $50 million.
The Mercantile Bank of the Americas, which had maintained its branches in South America, created new
offices in Paris, Barcelona, Berlin, and Madrid, and
financed direct trade between South America and Europe.
With the cooperation of the government, the Allied
blacklist caused the destruction of German banking
firms in Brazil. That contributed to an increase of
80 per cent in United States exports to Brazil, and the
NCB established a branch in Porto Alegre in 1918.
American financial progress elsewhere in Latin America
came from new business resulting from the war rather
than from closing German banks. British observers
agreed that shrewd and somewhat reckless business practices had given American banks a hold on most of this
new business and threatened the further growth of
British banks in that region.[8]

The wartime increase in trade between Asia and the
United States, and the resulting demand for dollar

---

[8]"American Banking in South American Markets,"
Bankers Magazine (London), September 1919, p. 278-283.
"Anglo-Argentine Banking," Bankers Magazine (London),
August 1918, p. 111. For a quick summary of the Ameri-
can banking position at the end of the war see
"America's World-Wide Banking Facilities," The World
Markets, August 1919. The war blacklists and diplomacy
destroyed German banking in Brazil but not elsewhere
in South America.

exchange, led to the formation in 1918 of the Asia
Banking Corporation with branches in Peking, Hankow,
Harbin, Shanghai, and Tientsin. The interest of West
Coast and mid-West banks in the Far East led to an in-
crease in the capital of this bank from $2 million to
$5 million in 1919. American and Canadian interests
organized the Park-Union Foreign Banking Corporation of
New York with capital of $2 million (and a surplus of
$250,000) to finance trade with Japan, China, and the
Dutch East Indies.[9]

While these numerous developments strengthened
American foreign banking for short-term trade finance,
the postwar problems of the United States and the
world promised to make even greater demands upon long-
term capital. This was anticipated by a National City
Bank officer early in 1919. "We cannot take part in
the reconstruction of Europe on sixty and ninety days
time. The exporters and banks cannot carry these credits.
They would soon be loaded up and out of the business."[10]
American bankers understood this, but their fear of
taking what they considered to be undue risks in Europe

---

[9]Commercial and Financial Chronicle, 7 June 1919,
p. 2298.

[10]George L. Roberts, "A Creditor Country," (pamphlet) quoted in the London Economist, 1 March 1919,
p. 361. For a similar opinion expressed by the Guaranty
Trust Company, see New York Times, 15 February 1921,
p. 22.

constrained their otherwise firm determination to take
a leading part in European reconstruction with long-
term investments. Once again, the investment bankers
wanted some assurances of protection from the United
States government before they made long-term commitments
abroad.[11] While not flatly opposed to the bankers'
plans, the government policies contrasted with those of
the financiers, and in the end served to discourage
them. During the time that Wall Street looked to Washington for a definite program, the net outflow of
private long-term capital, which had declined from
$790 million in 1915 to $396 million in 1918, promised
to decline still further in 1919.[12]

Outgoing Secretary William G. McAdoo set Treasury
policy upon the conclusion of the Armistice early in
November 1918 in a letter to the Chairman of the Senate
Finance Committee.[13] McAdoo called for the reduction
and eventual termination of government loans to Europe.

---

[11]New York Times, 1 December 1918, p. 9.

[12]Historical Statistics of the United States, p. 564.

[13]NARS, RG59, William Gibbs McAdoo to Senator
Furnifold McLendel Simmons. The Treasury was actually
fighting for a liberalization of a House appropriations
bill proposing drastic cuts in United States Government
loans abroad. McAdoo to Claude Kitchin (chairman,
House Ways and Means Committee), 5 December 1918, NARS,
RG56, Leffingwell Letter Press Copies, Volume 18, p. 476.
Also New York Times, 25 February 1919, p. 4.

He warned, though, of serious consequences for the
United States domestic economy should Congress act
suddenly. As a result, the Fifth Liberty Loan bill
provided for the extension to foreign governments of
credits to the amount of $1.5 billion, the extension of
maturity dates of foreign obligations owed to the
United States, and established a War Finance Corporation to make long-term loans to exporters and bankers
for one year after the war to facilitate the exportation
of domestic products.[14] The bill reflected the nation's
desire to end its spiraling debt, and to remove the
government from the money market, while at the same
time doing so in a way that would not precipitate a
crisis. Treasury officials felt private enterprise
would do the necessary business to prevent a dollar
shortage in Europe.

The Treasury Department was somewhat dismayed,
therefore, when the bankers did not support a policy of
private aid for Europe. Frank Vanderlip of the National
City Bank was one of the first and most prominent bankers to tour Europe following the war, and he expressed
that view to European financial leaders and to the
general public in his hastily written book, What

---

[14]New York Times, 25 February 1919, p. 4. Also
65th Congress, 3rd Session, House, Hearings on Fifth
Liberty Bond Bill (Washington: USGPO, 1919), pp. 35-43.

Happened in Europe.[15] Vanderlip felt that Europe needed
large amounts of long-term capital, but argued that the
American investing public would not supply the funds
because it did not know how to evaluate European stocks
and bonds. Reconstruction left in the hands of the
private banks worried him. He felt they would emphasize
loans offering the greatest security when "it may be
and probably is, more important first to make certain
loans where only the poorest security could be obtained."
Therefore, he favored the formation of a consortium of
international bankers, appointed and backed by the
governments of the United States and other important
nations exporting to Europe. The consortium, Vanderlip explained vaguely, would calculate the exact needs
of European nations and finance them accordingly.[16]
This call for government involvement upset the Treasury,
but many New York bankers who toured Europe and saw the
destruction came to agree with him in varying degrees.

---

[15]Norman H. Davis to Woodrow Wilson, 25 June 1919.
Also Carter Glass to Davis, 24 June 1919, Norman H.
Davis Papers, Box 11, Library of Congress.

[16]Frank Vanderlip, What Happened in Europe (New
York: MacMillan, 1919), passim. Vanderlip sent a memo
on his plan for an international loan to the Treasury
Department and made a general effort to publicize it.
The Treasury regarded the several plans for European
reconstruction which emerged in 1919 and 1920 as mere
variants on Vanderlip's. Norman H. Davis to Colonel
Edward House, 29 April 1919, Norman H. Davis Papers,
Box 160, Library of Congress.

This group included Paul Warburg, Henry P. Davison (of
Morgan & Company), Fred Kent of the Bankers' Trust Company, and Herbert Hoover, who, though not a banker,
exerted great influence at Paris as Director-General
of Relief for the Allies. Davison repeatedly argued
at Paris that, in order to give relief to Europe and
promote American trade, the demands of Europe must be
coordinated with the financial and industrial supplies
of the United States "throughout the whole country."
These views increased the urgency of the informal
financial discussions which developed spontaneously
between Americans and Europeans at Versailles.[17]

Somewhat surprisingly, President Wilson and his
numerous advisors had not emphasized the importance of
financial problems in formulating their plans for a
European settlement and were not prepared to meet the
demands made upon them at the outset of the conference.
Colonel Edward House and his academic inquiry unit,
entrusted by the President with the technical details
of anticipated Treaty problems, did not deal with
financial matters. But when House arrived in Paris,
financial problems immediately pressed in upon him and
he began cabling the President regarding the importance

[17]Commercial and Financial Chronicle, 14 June 1919,
p. 2397.

of financial and economic questions. According to a
Treasury representative at the Conference, the American
delegation realized by early December 1918 "that any
political or geographical arrangements would be useless
without harmonious financial and economic arrangements."[18]
Upon his arrival, Wilson perceived the importance of the
subject and, without formally abandoning Treasury policy
that "there can be no proper basis for a discussion of
our foreign loans in connection with the Peace Conference," cabled Secretary Glass that "it will be very
serviceable to have someone in whom you have the utmost
confidence sent over here to represent you in these
important matters."[19] Assistant Secretary of Treasury
Norman H. Davis, already in Europe for the express purpose of bringing Director-General Hoover to accept
Treasury policy, remained to become one of Wilson's
closest advisors at the Conference.[20] In addition,
the Treasury sent Thomas W. Lamont (Morgan and Company)
to advise the President on finance.

---

[18]Federal Records Center, Arlington, Virginia,
World War I Records, Bureau of Accounts, Box 104,
draft memo, 22 October 1918. Also Ibid., Allyn A.
Young to George May (Treasury Department), 12 November
1918 and Norman H. Davis to Russell C. Leffingwell,
2 December 1918.

[19]Woodrow Wilson to Carter Glass, 23 December
1918, NARS, RG56, Secretary file.

[20]Glass to Wilson, 2 January 1919, Norman H. Davis
Papers, Box 11, Library of Congress. Also Woodrow

The financial advisors first had to contend with
the proposal of the Allied governments to cancel the
wartime debts or, drawing on the wealth of the United
States in some other way, to dispose of the debts which
they felt would create a shortage of dollars and ruin
international trade. The British government pressed
insistently for a plan devised by their economic expert,
John M. Keynes, to place the United States in the
position of financing Europe's debts to the United
States by guaranteeing Germany's reparations obligations to the Allies. Wilson rejected that approach,
as his advisors suggested, on the grounds that it would
load American money markets with tax free bonds, reduce
revenue, depreciate the market for Liberty Bonds, and
lower the value of the dollar. All of those results
were contrary to Treasury Department policy. The
Treasury representatives instead advised the French and
British to keep their reparations demands low. That
would allow Germany to accumulate capital, rehabilitate

Wilson to Bainbridge Colby, 2 April 1920, Bainbridge
Colby Papers, Library of Congress. FRC WWI Records,
Bureau of Accounts, Box 104, Peace Commission, Albert
Strauss to Rathbone, 21 February 1919. Davis, Lamont,
Bernard Baruch, Vance McCormick, and Herbert Hoover are
reported to have been economic advisors to Wilson. For
Lamont's Treasury connection see R. C. Leffingwell to
Letter Press copies, Volume 18, p. 489. For Lamont's
influence at Versailles, see Thomas Lamont to J. P.
Morgan, 11 April 1919, Polk Papers, file on League
Cables, Library of Congress.

its economy, and help stabilize the European economy.[21]
The outcome was an *impasse* on financial matters that
threatened to prolong European economic instability.
President Wilson became increasingly concerned. In
April 1919, after the heaviest pressure from political
matters had passed, he directed his financial advisors
to give their private, unofficial attention to the
problem of reconstruction. He promised that Vanderlip's
proposals for a consortium would receive serious consideration.[22]

After various American delegates hastily appraised
European conditions, Lamont prepared a four-point
analysis of the crucial financial requirements. This
included:

1. Credits to be advanced to the newly
constructed states of Poland, Czechoslovakia, Greater Serbia, Rumania, and
the Baltic States for the establishment
of stable currencies, the purchase of
raw materials, and of transportation
and agricultural equipment.
2. Refunding or cancelling of interest on
loans to allied governments for three
or five years.

[21]Seth P. Tillman, Anglo-American Relations at the
Paris Peace Conference of 1919 (Princeton, Princeton
University Press, 1961), p. 271. Davis to Albert Rath-
bone (Treasury), 24 April 1919, Norman Davis Papers,
Box 16a, Library of Congress. Wilson rejected the
Keynes plan in a note written by Davis and Lamont. Ibid.

[22]Colonel Edward House to Norman H. Davis, 5 May
1919, Davis Papers, Box 16a, Library of Congress.
Peace Negotiations Memoranda, 21 April 1919, Bernard
Baruch Papers, Princeton University Library.

3. Credits for raw materials for France,
    Belgium, and Italy.
4. Working capital for Germany and the
    enemy states to enable them to resume
    their industrial life and, ultimately,
    to make reparations payments.[23]

Lamont tried to satisfy the Treasury by proposing "to

handle everything possible through private channels."

At the same time, Lamont and others wanted the

United States government to take more initiative and

the recommendations to Washington tried to pressure

Wilson by creating a sense of urgency calling for special

measures.[24] This was especially clear in the proposals

that the United States allow the War Finance Corporation

to guarantee export credits and thus relieve the

exporters. Though a consortium of European banks would

be created to support European importers, Davis and

Lamont feared that "American exporters would not take

even this slight risk" and would refuse to export.

They also called on the Treasury Department to re-

fund the interest due on foreign obligations, and to

work with a special committee of private American

interests to coordinate the reconstruction effort in

the United States. In return for such government aid,

the United States should demand that no preferential

---

[23]Norman Davis and Thomas Lamont to R. C. Leffingwell (Treasury), 27 May 1919, Davis Papers, Box 16a,
Library of Congress.

[24]Ibid.

tariffs be established in Europe that discriminated
against American nationals, and prevent exclusive con-
cessions working against American interests.[25]

Lamont and Davis went so far as to discuss with
Davison the possibility of mobilizing and coordinating
private credit resources in America. By June, the
offices of Morgan and Company had become the center of
a private reconstruction plan that Davison described as
"entirely inclusive. If it is adopted it will include
all the banking and industrial forces of the entire
country." Davison called for bankers to cooperate
closely with industrial units and extend credits to
European purchasers, and to finance them by issuing
debentures to the American public. The United States
Government would take 10 per cent of all the debentures
issued by the underwriters against the credits they
advanced for foreign purchases. "This seems to be a
necessary arrangement," said one banker, "for with the
government participant the debentures will be considerably more attractive than otherwise." This plan,
endorsed by the Federal Reserve Board, was adopted at
a conference in June 1919 of the Board and the

---

[25]Ibid.

representatives of the bankers, producers, exporters,
and manufacturers involved.[26]

The Treasury regarded the estimates of Europe's
needs, from which demands for government assistance
sprung, as excessive, and found the source of these
estimates in the desire of industrial concerns to continue their wartime profits. Assistant Secretary of
Treasury Russell Leffingwell regarded a decline in
American exports as inevitable because the relative
shortage of dollar exchange made American goods increasingly expensive. As a result, the abnormal demand
would decline. Europe's production and trade would
increase until it could obtain goods from the United
States without borrowing. That course, he argued, would
free American production for the American market, which
would bring lower prices — and that in turn would lead
to the foreign expansion of American goods and finance
on a sound basis.

Understanding that those developments would cause
shocks to the international economy, the Treasury
Department approved some long-term private loans to the

[26]New York Times, 11 May 1919, p. 16. New York
Times, 4 June 1919, p. 20, 14 June 1919, p. 1. Commercial and Financial Chronicle, 21 June 1919, p. 2483.
At least one farmers organization opposed Davison's
plan. The Farmer's National Council wanted American
foreign investments put under the control of the
Federal government. Commercial and Financial Chronicle,
28 June 1919, p. 2583.

Allied debtors, and backed adequate private banking
credits to facilitate imports from Europe as well as
exports to Europe. Specifically, it approved the
National City Bank's plans for expansion. The Treasury
also desired to negotiate the refunding of the demand
obligations it held against the Allies into long-term
obligations. The United States Government offered
direct assistance to Europe through war surplus disposal,
the War Finance Corporation, and the Grain Corporation.
But further aid would only prolong the painful transition to a sound international economy.[27] The Treasury
Department therefore opposed all the proposals advanced
by the financial advisors in Paris.

Assistant Secretary Leffingwell described the
Davison plan as "a private monopoly of international
trade and finance which the Treasury will not stand
for."[28] The Treasury and the Federal Reserve Board ab-
horred the idea of guaranteeing export credits.[29] The
unilateral proposal to refund the interest obligations

---

[27]FRC, World War I Records, Box 105, Reconstruction-
European, 1918-1919, R. C. Leffingwell to Albert
Rathbone, 11 September 1919.

[28]FRC, World War I Records, Box 105, Leffingwell
note to Kelley, Davis, Strauss, and Rathbone (Treasury),
28 August 1919.

[29]NARS, RG56, Box 69, Foreign Trade, 1917-1919,
Leffingwell to Norman Davis, Memo, 17 October 1919.

would encourage the former Allies to hope for the cancellation of the debts and delay the settlement of reparations terms with Germany. "It is unfortunate but nevertheless true," Leffingwell concluded, "that public sentiment in this country is in no mood to tolerate the assumption by this Government of further financial burdens in aid of Europe."[30] These objections to the plan developed by Vanderlip, Lamont, Davis, and Davison persuaded the Federal Reserve Board, the Treasury, and eventually the Congress, to encourage instead the formation of federally incorporated investment trusts to finance American exports.

Such firms would take foreign securities in payment for exports and reimburse the exporters with funds gathered through the sale of debentures issued to the investing public against the foreign securities. This was something like Henry Davison's scheme, but it was more decentralized, financially and administratively. The Federal Reserve Board and the Federal Advisory Council decided to press for the adoption of the federal incorporation amendment in June 1919. Federal Reserve lawyers used an earlier Senate bill in which they made a few adjustments and, with the endorsement of the

_____

[30]There is evidence that Leffingwell himself would have preferred permission for a stronger program from Congress. See Leffingwell to Davis, 6 May 1919, NARS, RG56, WFC, 1919-1922.

Treasury Department, gave it to Senator Walter Edge of
New Jersey. The Edge Act met the requirements of the
bankers and the government, making scarce financial
skills generally available, diversifying risk, and
encouraging investors by giving the trusts "the moral
backing and material support of the United States
Government."[31]

As Edge told the Senate, "Every step in the transaction would be under the supervision of the United
States through the Federal Reserve Board...such investments would be thoroughly safeguarded..." "If this is
not done," warned Senator Robert Owen of the Senate
Banking Committee, "we are going to meet with an ob-
struction to our foreign commerce that will react with
the most injurious consequences upon the people of the
United States, upon the home markets, and upon all sorts
of stocks and securities."[32] Edge's bill stipulated
that the investment trusts had to have a minimum

---

[31]Walter Edge, quoted in the Commercial and Finan-
cial Chronicle, 28 June 1919, p. 2583. For the
background of the bill see Ibid., and Charles Hamlin
Diary, Volume 5, 20 June 1919, Library of Congress.
Also Federal Reserve Bulletin, July 1919, p. 611. Also
Richard Owen, "The $100,000,000 Foreign Trade Financing
Corporation," Journal of Political Economy, January
1932. Also United States House of Representatives,
66th Congress, /no session specified7, Edge Act
Hearings.

[32]Commercial and Financial Chronicle, 23 August
1919, p. 732.

capitalization of $7 million, and the bankers themselves estimated that such corporations could market their debentures and make advances to foreign importers at a ratio of $6 to $1 of capitalization. Congress reduced the minimum capitalization to $2 million. Upon the passage of the Edge Act in 1919, the American Bankers' Association, the United States Chamber of Commerce, and the National Foreign Trade Council launched an organizing campaign for the formation of a $100 million foreign trade bank.[33]

Bankers and exporters resisted the administration's willingness to see the export trade decline (especially with Europe) and threatened that hard times would come if that happened.[34] Reports from Europe during the summer of 1919 were pessimistic and the need for American goods seemed genuine. Vanderlip openly predicted the collapse of the continent unless the United States provided massive aid.[35] Edward R. Stettinius (of Morgan and Company) felt that the United States should not only support European reconstruction with its influence but with its credit.[36] In conversations

[33]Chapter VI, below.

[34]New York Times, 9 September 1919, p. 23.

[35]FRC, World War I Records, Box 105, Strong to Leffingwell, 31 August 1919.

[36]NYFRB, Strong Diary, 28 July 1919.

with London bankers, Benjamin Strong of the New York
Federal Reserve Bank learned that they also felt that
European reconstruction depended upon American assistance, although they did not want cancellation of the
wartime debts.[37] Hoover took a very gloomy view of the
situation. Persuaded to the Treasury Department
policy earlier in the year, he now favored direct government aid to Europe, and cabled Wilson to invite
European finance ministers to Washington as a way of
awakening America to Europe's peril.[38]

A general willingness to sell permeated the financial, manufacturing, and merchant population and
pushed the favorable balance of trade in 1919 to a
record of nearly $5 billion. This was nearly 50 per
cent higher than it had been (in terms of value) in
1917, the biggest export year of the war.[39] Government assistance financed more than 40 per cent of the

---

[37]Ibid., 24 July 1919. Ibid., 30 August 1919.
Strong gradually came to favor increased government aid
of a stop-gap character, provided especially through a
bigger Grain Corporation to sell meat and fats, as
well as grain, on long-term credit. He also called for
more credit through the War Finance Corporation to
direct banking and investment funds towards industrial
reconstruction.

[38]Ibid., 29 July 1919. Hoover was consistently
critical of the administration's estimates of Europe's
needs. For some of his views see Herbert Hoover to
Norman Davis, 16 May 1919, Box 16a, Norman H. Davis
Papers, Library of Congress.

[39]Historical Statistics, p.566 . Some of the
increase in acceptance liabilities derived from special

total. One-fifth came from remittances by immigrants.
Bankers acceptances increased rapidly to about $1.3
billion of which $641 million was still outstanding at
the end of the year. This accounted for another one-
fifth of the favorable balance of trade. Open book
credits of merchants and manufacturers accounted for
the remaining approximately $730 million. A large pro-
portion of that sum was lost in the liquidation of the
following year, if the statements by bankers can be
taken at face value.[40]

Bankers felt the lack of government protection for
long-term investments, and wanted a "sound foreign
policy on this point."[41] The predominance of short-
term financial arrangements revealed the obvious
reluctance of long-term capital to venture to Europe.
There were notable exceptions. Morgan and Company,

---

efforts by large interests. A syndicate of New York
bankers established a $25 million credit to finance
cotton for mills in Czechoslovakia. Another group
handled a similar credit to Poland. Morgan and Company,
in an effort to capture what it regarded as the desirable Belgian market, established a $50 million credit
for Belgian financial interests.

[40]See Chapter VI, below.

[41]New York Times, 14 July, 1919, p. 15. Fred Kent
felt the United States' Mexican policy was a great
drawback to healthy reconstruction "because it has placed
great fear in the minds of foreign interests as to our
attitude toward anarchy." Fred Kent to Seward Prosser
(Guaranty Trust Company), 28 August 1919, Box 1, Miscellaneous letters, Kent Papers, Princeton University
Library.

acting with New York's biggest banks, pooled $10 million
to form the First Foreign Corporation, an investment
trust that could issue debentures to raise additional
capital against accumulated holdings.[42] Three foreign
banking corporations, the Asia Banking Corporation, the
American Foreign Banking Corporation, and the Mercantile Bank of the Americas, formed the Foreign Bond and
Share Corporation, a $3 million investment trust.[43]
But because the managers of this corporation were
heavily involved in Asia and Latin America, and were
distrustful of European financial stability, they
planned to channel their funds into underdeveloped
countries. For the third year since 1916 the over-all
commitment of private American long-term funds dropped
— to $169 million.[44]

The United States Chamber of Commerce lent its
weight to demands for government support. It sponsored
a meeting between leading industrialists, New York
banking and investment houses, and the officials of
devastated French towns and cities. John Foster Dulles

[42]New York Times, 22 November, 1919, p. 22.

[43]Commercial and Financial Chronicle, 26 April 1919,
p. 1664. NARS, RG40, File 640, Maurice Hutchinson, vice
president of Foreign Bond and Share, to B. S. Cutler,
chief, Bureau of Foreign and Domestic Commerce, 10 June
1919.

[44]Historical Statistics, p. 564.

alerted the Treasury that the meeting was called to de-
vise a reconstruction plan for France that would
eliminate Germany's responsibilities. That was contrary
to United States policy.[45] The Treasury dispatched its
sole remaining Paris agent to the meeting to warn that
France's needs were much exaggerated, and to encourage
swift ratification of the Peace Treaty in order to
stabilize Europe and prepare the way for the free flow
of American capital. Benjamin Strong also promoted the
Treasury Department brand of realism at the meeting.
Restrain credit and thereby promote a reparations and
peace settlement, he urged, and then suggested that the
War Finance Corporation and the enlarged Grain Corporation supply short-term solutions to the immediate
problems. "If through these sources $1.5 to $2.0 billion
could be furnished in the next six to eight months," he
concluded, "it would give us...needed influence to
insist on a settlement of many pending disputes and I
believe the peril of the winter situation would be
largely removed."

The influence of the Treasury Department, and its
constant reiteration of its policy wherever financiers
gathered, eventually impressed dissident American

[45]FRC, World War I Records, Box 105, Dulles to
Secretary of State Lansing, 27 July 1919.

bankers. In October, the United States Chamber of Commerce sponsored an International Trade Conference of European and American manufacturing and financial interests. The meeting affirmed Treasury Department policy. James Alexander, president of the National Bank of Commerce, and chairman of the Conference Committee on Credits and Finance, cleared his conference address with Assistant Secretary of Treasury Leffingwell. It revealed he was "in entire sympathy with the Treasury's position."[46] The resulting report of the committee on credit and finance reflected the Treasury Department's optimistic view of European conditions. According to the committee, Great Britain desired only to maintain existing credit and business relationships with the United States, and was not seeking any special arrangements. Belgium and Italy were reported to be making rapid progress in restoring normal conditions, and their banks were judged generally sound and operating with increased capital. These countries, and France, wanted sufficient credits to purchase raw materials, and asked terms of such length to permit them to resume exports.[47]

---

[46]FRC, World War I Records, Box 105, Leffingwell to Joseph P. Tumulty (secretary to the President of the United States), 23 October 1919.

[47]Report of the Committee on Credit and Finance, United States Chamber of Commerce International Trade Conference (New York, 1919), 20-24 October 1919, p. 296.

These views meant that much of the conference rhetoric
was devoted to reaffirming that Great Britain, Italy,
France and Belgium were economically sound, that their
securities had adequate backing to attract American
investors, and that they would repay the debts they had
contracted.[48]

Dwight Morrow of Morgan and Company outlined the
consequences of conference policy in terms reminiscent
of Treasury Department statements. "I believe," he
said, "that the turn has now come. I believe that the
exports from the United States to Europe must gradually
diminish and the imports from Europe must increase...
at a time when we are complaining of the high cost of
living we should welcome an increase of our imports of
those things that Europe can make for us better than
we can make them for ourselves."[49] Morrow estimated a
European trade deficit of about $2 billion for 1920.
As for the capital to finance this deficit, Morrow
suggested that the man of the hour was "not the manufacturer as such, nor the producer of raw material as
such, nor the banker as such, but the man who saves."
He was reluctant to develop this theme at the conference. Since export finance was the major theme of the

[48]Ibid.

[49]New York Times, 24 October 1919, p. 27.

conference, the Edge Act, then making its way through
the Congress, emerged as a golden hope because it
promised to solve the problem of attracting savings,
and providing government moral support, for export
trade finance.[50]

By the end of 1919, the Treasury Department could
conclude with some satisfaction that "opinion is
straightening out." The Federal Reserve Board observed
that the usual banking machinery was "beginning to
operate in a normal way," and that there was no reason
to doubt its adequacy in practically "caring for the
demands which grow out of the actual business of foreign
countries."[51] But pressure from Europe disrupted the
consensus that the Treasury Department had obtained
after many months of striving. Influential European
bankers expressed their dissatisfaction with "temporary
expedients" for finance adopted by the United States,
and complained of the lack of "positive direct progress
being made toward a coherent and consistent cleaning
up of the various financial messes produced by the war."

Developed by Paul Warburg and G. Vissering of the
Nederlandsche Bank, the Amsterdam plan, as it was known,

---

[50]Ibid., passim., especially pp. 201 and 269.

[51]FRC, Box 105, Edge Act and Correspondence file,
A. S. (Albert Strauss) to R. C. Leffingwell, memo with
Leffingwell's handwritten comment, 24 November 1919.

called for an international conference in Europe to study
the entire question of postwar finance. They hoped for
definite recommendations for action that would be presented to the various governments. Warburg privately
felt that England and the United States should release
some of their Allied debtors, and doubted that many of
the debts would ever be paid. "I consider it danger-
ous," he wrote the influential Treasury official Norman
Davis, "for the United States Government to be placed
in a position, very unfairly, of course, where it would
be considered the world usurer."[52] Fred I. Kent,
formerly of the Treasury Department, endorsed the plan
for fear that, without some encouragement from the
United States, the neutral nations would withdraw and
abort the project. He immediately contacted the
Treasury Department, which informed him of its opposition. He retracted his endorsement.[53]

Despite this episode and other opposition from the
Treasury Department, the bankers prepared a memorial

---

[52]FRC, World War I Records, Box 128, Warburg to
Norman Davis, 26 November 1919.

[53]Ibid., Glass to Rathbone, 13 November 1919.
Kent to Warburg, 2 December 1919, Kent Papers, Princeton
University Library. Kent to Vissering, 10 November
1919, Kent Papers, Princeton. Kent nevertheless felt
that the Amsterdam meeting had been a success because
the subsequent action would reveal "whether the government of the United States is willing to be approached
at the moment with the idea of making advances to
Europe."

for presentation to the governments. They included broad proposals for "reviving and maintaining international commerce." The memorial called for countries having favorable trade balances to supply funds to debtor nations. In deference to the Treasury Department's objections, Warburg deleted from the American draft of the memorial the phrase recommending that the wartime debts be forgiven. But that call was retained in European drafts.[54] From the United States Treasury's point of view, however subtly and indirectly it was phrased, the memorial advanced the unacceptable idea that the United States should give assistance to Europe in the form of surrendering existing loans, deferring existing loans, or making new loans.[55] A conference called on the basis of this idea "would arouse false hopes" since, in the view of Treasury, no government could be a party to such a conference without strengthening the impression that the government contemplated or favored direct governmental financial action. The Treasury opposed this form of action and felt that any encouragement would lead to a delay in the application

---

[54]"History of the European Memorandum," (typed mss.) Post War Europe file, Warburg Papers, Yale University Library.

[55]FRC, World War I Records, Box 126 (Warburg Memorial), Leffingwell memo of conversation with Warburg, 8 and 9 January 1920. Also Ibid., Leffingwell to Glass, 30 January 1920 (memo).

of effective remedies for the European financial situation. Those panaceas were hard work, high taxes, low
reparations, and the ratification of a Peace Treaty.

The Amsterdam proposal nevertheless commanded great
support in the American business community. By December 1919, when the bankers presented it to the Secretary
of the Treasury in its final form, the United States
Chamber of Commerce and nearly every influential banking house in the country had endorsed it.[56] The final
draft attempted to relieve the government of any
official connection with the proposed conference by
suggesting that the Chamber of Commerce designate delegates to the conference after an expression of official
approval from the Treasury. The Treasury rejected the
proposal entirely. Secretary Glass reiterated traditional policy. Economic aid for restoration must be
supplied through private channels, and that "as a
necessary contribution to that end, the governments of
the world should adopt sound financial policies."
The Secretary then concluded that if the Chamber of
Commerce considered it advisable and desirable to
designate representatives to attend an unofficial conference, the Treasury did not object "provided the

---

[56]Warburg Memorial (copy), 15 January 1920,
Warburg Papers, Yale University Library.

scope and character of such a conference as well as the
impossibility of United States government action are
clearly understood."[57]

Paul Warburg wrote Assistant Secretary Leffingwell
that Glass's statement had created an atmosphere of
coolness and aloofness. Leffingwell replied with yet
another reiteration of Treasury policy and concluded
that "your conference, now that the limitations upon
its scope are clearly stated can do no harm and may do
some good."[58] Treasury representatives in Europe were
informed that the Department did not oppose "an international conference to discuss financial and economic
questions," but that it was opposed to sending American
representatives, official or unofficial, to any conference to discuss "to whom and by whom loans should be
made, and to consider deflating international balance
sheets by the cancellation of intergovernmental indebt-
edness."[59] The bankers, lamenting the lack of "positive
impetus" from Washington, pessimistically arranged the

[57]FRC, World War I Records, Box 128, Secretary
Carter Glass to Homer Furgeson (President, United States
Chamber of Commerce), 23 January 1920. The same letter
appears in the Federal Reserve Bulletin, February 1920,
p. 137.

[58]FRC, World War I Records, Box 128, Leffingwell
to Warburg, 4 February 1920.

[59]Ibid., Norman Davis to Albert Rathbone,
27 March 1930.

conference for the fall of 1920 at Brussels,
Belgium.[60]

---

[60]Ibid., Warburg to Leffingwell, 4 February 1920.

Chapter VI
Contraction and Consolidation

While the Wilson administration was quite interested in the Brussels Conference of October 1920 as an
opportunity to win European acceptance of United States
policy, the Treasury Department hesitated to become too
directly or enthusiastically involved for fear of im-
plying government aid for European recovery. The
evidence indicates that there was some desire to send
an impressive unofficial delegation to the conference.
But, in the end, the Department selected only Roland W.
Boyden, an unofficial representative on the League of
Nations' reparations commission, to represent the
United States.[1] In his address, Boyden repeated the
administration's "no loan" policy and stressed the need
for greater economic cooperation among the European
states to improve stability and insure American confidence in Europe. Some of the European press commented
bitterly on Boyden's remarks. "Evidently the attitude

---

[1]_Foreign Relations of the United States_, Volume I,
1920, p. 95, /551.A1/40a_/ Secretary of State Colby to
/?_/ Wallace (Ambassador to France), 17 September 1920.
A search of Treasury and State Department files failed
to reveal the basis for the decision to reduce the
importance of the American delegation.

of the United States...proves," Le Temps noted, "that
the principle of international solidarity in financial
and economic matters is not understood by all in the
same manner."[2] But the response of the convention
delegates, most of them financiers of high standing,
revealed that they were resigned to American policy
and ready to adopt drastic measures to stabilize the
European economy. And, despite the undertones of
accusation, the American ambassador was pleased to
report that "no real drive" was made to punish the United
States for its unyielding financial policy.[3]

The nature of the problems confronting the delegates also helped produce an agreement on a sound
course of action. The conference unanimously endorsed
a long list of austerity measures to restore fiscal
responsibility in European states, and to channel
savings into most useful production. Once Europe had
restored its export trade to the United States, the
difficult problem of obtaining dollar exchange with
which to purchase American goods would be solved. But
that was at best a long run solution, and meanwhile the

[2]New York Times, 30 September 1920, p. 24.

[3]Foreign Relations of the United States, Volume I,
1920, p. 102, 551.A1/53, Brand Whitlock (Ambassador to
Belgium) for Roland W. Boyden to Norman H. Davis and
David Houston, 9 October 1920.

reconstruction of Europe seemed to require immediate
supplies of scarce dollar credit. Even countries that
were not credit risks, like Norway and Sweden, paid
8% interest. Loans to other nations, even if available,
would in all likelihood be at prohibitive rates.[4]

For this reason, American and European observers
felt that the Brussels Conference made its greatest
contribution in adopting a plan to attract private
international movements of capital that was devised by
Dr. Ter Meulen of Holland. Under this plan, each government would issue bonds against the gold value of the
nation's basic assets. An exporter granting credit
would hold the bonds in appropriate amounts until he
received payment from the importer, who would then
accept the bonds from the exporter and return them to
the government. The borrowing nations had the responsibility for initiating action, which began by notifying
the central organization of creditors what assets were
going to be pledged for credit.

The conditions established by the organization
required each country to balance its budget promptly,
stop printing paper money, and lower tariff barriers

---

[4]Commercial and Financial Chronicle, 2 October
1920, p. 1305. Federal Reserve Bulletin, December
1920, p. 1277.

on important imports and exports.[5] "The most efficient
assistance," a spokesman for the plan declared, "could
be extended by the American investor through investment in Edge Act banks." Those institutions would hold
the Ter Meulen bonds as security and issue debentures
against their value. "All that is needed," he concluded,
"is liberal support of these credit instruments to
thoroughly and fully revive foreign trade."[6] But the
Ter Meulen arrangements required time because of the
necessity for elaborate assessments of proffered
securities by a special League of Nations commission.
As a result, the plan delayed long-term credit to
Europe, and helped to undermine the organization of the
Edge Act banks.

The enthusiasm for organizing Edge Act corporations, manifested by members and manufacturers after
the passage of the Act in December 1919, collapsed in
the face of the serious difficulties created by the
domestic demand for goods and capital, and because of
the lack of firm business opportunities in Europe. From
the start of the organizational effort for a $100,000,000
trade bank by the American Banking Association, Governor

---

[5]*Commercial and Financial Chronicle*, 20 November
1920, pp. 1998-1999.

[6]*New York Times*, 2 November 1921, p. 27.

Harding of the Federal Reserve System predicted slow
going for the project because of the general shortage
of capital.[7] To overcome this weakness, at least to
some extent, the Federal Reserve System had planned from
the beginning to use the War Finance Corporation to
help the Edge Act investment trusts by allowing it to
subscribe heavily to their debentures. The corporations would "very naturally" come to the War Finance
Corporation and seek a subscription to a particular
issue of debentures. The War Finance Corporation might
subscribe up to 20 per cent, and that was expected to
have "a good moral effect" because it would show that
the government of the United States had confidence in
the proposition. That would, in turn, enable the bond
selling organization to place the balance of the loans
with the public. "And in that way," according to
Governor Harding, "the $1 billion that the War Finance
Corporation may invest will go a very long way."[8]

---

[7]W. P. G. Harding address to Massachusetts Bankers
Association, quoted in Commercial and Financial
Chronicle, 10 January 1920, p. 119.

[8]W. P. G. Harding, speech to United States Chamber
of Commerce International Trade Conference, 24 October
1919, p. 278. The WFC intended to play an important
role in the formation of Edge Act banks from the outset. NARS, RG56, War Finance Corporation, George L.
Harrison to /Albert7 Strauss, 2 October 1919. In a
penciled note at the bottom of the letter Leffingwell
wrote to Eugene Meyer of the WFC, "It is very important
to be sure of this." Meyer replied, "I have never had
any doubt on this point."

In spite of those intentions, the War Finance Corporation played no part in the implementation of the
Edge Act. At the same time that the Federal Reserve
Board earnestly began to contract credit in May 1920,
the Treasury Department terminated the War Finance Corporation. A Chicago banker and Federal Reserve Bank
advisor explained that they "had it up with the Secretary /Glass7, and we agreed with him that a little
pressure was necessary...and that was part of the
pressure."[9] Almost immediately, agricultural interests
suffering from sharp declines in prices exerted pressure in the Congress for the renewal of the Finance
Corporation in order to increase their exports. Over
the bitter opposition of the administration, the Congress restored it in January 1921. Of the total
advances made by the corporation during the year 1921,
$51 million (or about one-third) was used to finance
otherwise desperate commodity exports, and about two-
thirds of that involved cotton of the lowest grades.
But the War Finance Corporation made no loans to Edge

---

[9]James B. Forgan (chairman of the board of the
First National Bank of Chicago), United States House
of Representatives, 66th Congress, Third Session,
Hearings Before the Committee on Banking and Currency
on S. J. 212, War Finance Corporation (Washington,
U.S.G.P.O.), p. 58.

Act Corporations.[10]

The force of the American Bankers Association
campaign caused several states to pass legislation
allowing their state-chartered banks to subscribe to
stock in the proposed $100,000,000 trade bank. Member
banks of the Association were encouraged to subscribe
6 per cent of their capital and surplus to the gigantic
scheme. In general, western cities of the nation
exhibited the greatest interest in promoting the corporation and contributed the greatest amount of funds.
Organization was handicapped, however, by the failure
of the Association to clarify what the corporation was
going to do, and to explain the kinds of foreign
securities it would accept as collateral for its
loans.[11] Some potential participants feared that the
venture would become involved in financing the export

---

[10]In the bitter struggle of the renewal of the
WFC, Eugene Meyer, Jr., charged that the termination of
the first WFC was responsible for the failure of the
Edge Act banks to develop. Ibid., Part 3, p. 75.
For a summary of activities of the War Finance Corpora-
tion see Woodbury Willoughby, The Capital Issues
Committee and the War Finance Corporation, The John
Hopkins University Studies in Historical and Political
Science, Volume 52 (Baltimore: John Hopkins, 1924),
p. 93.

[11]New York Times, 1 April 1921, p. 21. For a
general summary of the problems of Edge Act organization see Richard N. Owen, "The $100,000,000 Foreign
Trade Financing Corporation," Journal of Political
Economy, January 1922, p. 359-361.

balances of 1919 which were still outstanding on short-
term account. They were skeptical; the goods were
sustaining heavy losses while off the market in foreign
warehouses while world prices tumbled.

None of the big Chicago banks subscribed to the
corporation. They felt that the proposed organization
was too large and its plans too vague. In addition,
the Ter Meulen scheme encouraged a wait-and-see attitude. "We think it would be well," concluded
influential Chicago leaders, "to wait until the cooperation of this commission /of the League of Nations7
can be secured."[12] Those obstacles, along with the
general slump in business and the downward trend of
foreign exchange, so hampered the Foreign Trade Finance
Corporation's efforts to accumulate the required amount
of capital that the organization abandoned the project
in January 1922.[13] The demise of that $100,000,000
corporation marked the end of the large scale plans
for raising capital for reconstruction.

---

[12]New York Times, 10 February 1921, p. 17. Also
Owen, op. cit. A good presentation of the Chicago
point of view was George M. Reynolds' (chairman of
the board, Continental and Commercial National Bank,
Chicago), "Capital, Shall We Export It or Use It for
American Business?" in The Annals of the American
Academy of Political and Social Science, September
1921, passim.

[13]New York Times, 21 January 1922, p. 18.

The economic environment of 1920 exerted a great effect on the international economy throughout the post-war years. Europe in particular suffered the loss of many of its pre-war markets because of the rise of effective competition during the war years. Japan had increased its exports to Asia by 125 per cent, to South America by 629 per cent, and to Africa by 1,002 per cent.[14] The United States had made immense gains in trade with South America, Canada, and Asia. The important Russian market was, to a large extent, blocked to European development and trade. The German industrial machine, not seriously damaged by the war, faced difficult competition, particularly in the important metals trade, from the United States. Great Britain learned that the war had so stimulated the development of engineering and industry in France that the two nations, which formerly supplemented each other economically, had become rivals.[15] The wartime growth of small industry in some developing nations threatened to cut the exports of industrialized nations

[14]Kukujiro Yamasaki and Gotaro Ogawa, Effect of the War on the Commerce and Industry of Japan, Economic and Social History of the World War, Japanese Series (New Haven: Yale University Press, 1929), p. 10.

[15]Paul Mantoux, "Trade with France Before and After the War," Journal of the Royal Statistical Society, May 1917, p. 383-407.

and reduce the market. India and Japan increased their production of cotton textiles, for example, and Japan became an important exporter of that commodity to Asian markets.[16] The production of steel increased tremendously throughout Asia during the war years. Brazil, Chile, and Argentina initiated expensive efforts to develop their textile and shoe industries. And all developing countries raised high tariff walls to protect new industries after the conclusion of the war.[17]

Under these and related conditions, the economic union of the Allies that had been planned during the period of wartime solidarity proved impossible to create or maintain. Germany had been the largest market for French exports and the second most important source of France's imports. Discrimination against Germany would hurt French trade and damage the possibility of reparations payments from the former enemy. Tariff preferences limited to former Allies would involve abandoning the most-favored nation clause and terminating trade contacts with neutrals upon which both Great Britain and France relied. Moreover, such policies

---

[16]Francis W. Hirst, The Consequences of the War to Great Britain, Economic and Social History of the World War, British Series (London: Humphrey Milford Oxford University Press, New Haven: Yale University Press, 1934), p. 265 and p. 273.

[17]Ibid., p. 266.

might drive neutral countries into an economic alliance
with the former enemy powers and precipitate the creation of an economic Mittel-Europa, contrary to the
fixed policy of the Western powers.[18]

Without a program for world, or even regional,
cooperation, European nations fell back on the pro-
tectionist policies of the pre-war period. The war
had emphasized the importance of self-sufficiency in
strategic materials, moreover, rather than encouraging
the troublesome and demanding policy of economic interdependence. This feeling intensified the attachment
to tariffs and encouraged Europe to raise the levels
considerably higher than they had been before the war.
As early as 1918, Great Britain planned tariff protection for many vital branches of production and the
development of an imperial trade network through
preferential tariffs to the members of the British
Commonwealth.[19] France also adopted strictly national
and imperial policies in industry and commerce,
designing its tariffs to encourage trade with French
colonies and reduce other imports to an absolute
minimum.[20] These policies were in distinct conflict

---

[18]Frank Arnold Haight, A History of French Commercial Policies (MacMillan Company, New York, 1941),
p. 94-95.

[19]Ibid., p. 98.

[20]Ibid., p. 104.

with the American view of post-war international trade
expansion.

More serious in this respect were the problems of
dollar exchange which developed in 1919 and increased
thereafter. American support of the pound sterling
ceased immediately after the war. Shortly afterward,
the British and French governments withdrew their
support of sterling and franc exchange, and those currencies declined in value relative to the dollar.
American goods cost more in terms of francs and shil-
lings, and that further discouraged exports. But
behind the complications of foreign exchange and the
adverse effect on American trade lay the basic problem of prices. The devaluation of European currencies
did not cut those nations off from the world prices of
raw materials.[21] All other things being equal, if the
pound declined, it took more pounds to buy the same
quantity of raw materials. This inevitably forced the
price of the finished product higher unless the manufacturers cut costs in other stages of production.
Competitively, at least, the United States was no
worse off after the devaluation of the European currencies than before, except that American manufacturers

---

[21]Republished from "Bulletin Number 10," First
Federal Foreign Banking Association, New York City,
The Economic World, 18 June 1921, p. 873.

maintained their high wartime prices while European manufacturers showed a readiness to cut costs and prices to regain their lost markets.[22]

At the same time, Treasury pressure and the difficulties of financing trade to Europe caused an increasingly outspoken willingness on the part of American bankers to abandon extraordinary economic relationships with Europe. James Alexander (president of the National Bank of Commerce), who was close to the Treasury Department, told the American Manufacturers Export Association in October 1920 that "it is one of the pre-eminent duties of the banks to encourage a return as fast as possible to reciprocal foreign trade equilibrium financed by local credits. If a marked recession of our export trade should prove to be one of the corrective factors tending to stabilize international trade...such a recession should be accepted as economically sound."[23] Thomas W. Lamont encouraged the same group to think of the Far East: "The greatest foreign outlet in the world for American manufacturers

---

[22]Ibid., p. 874. Paul Warburg to Sir Henry Strakosch, /?/ 1920, Warburg Papers, Yale University. The Belgians, who managed to obtain a $50 million credit in the United States, used only a small portion because they found American prices too high. NYPRB, Strong Diary, 5 August 1919.

[23]James S. Alexander, "Why We Must Have Foreign Trade," Address at the Ninth National Foreign Trade Council, 10 May 1922 (pamphlet).

and enterprise.[24] In the spring of 1920, the manager
of the powerful Foreign Department of the Guaranty Trust
Corporation told the American Manufacturers Export
Association that "it is natural that our exports should
be curtailed to those countries which are no longer
able to make payment in the form in which we demand
payment...The American exporter should turn to the Far
East and South America." "Our exporters have been
concentrating far too much of their attention," he
argued, "upon Europe itself."[25] The abandonment of
the Edge Act banks underlined this view.

The foreign trade of the United States paralleled
this rhetoric to a marked degree in 1920. Exports to
Europe declined by about 20 per cent, but increased to
every other region of the world. Though the value of
Europe's imports from the United States was annually
3 times greater than in pre-war years, its proportion
of the American export trade declined by 6.5 per cent.[26]

---

[24]James S. Alexander, address to the Eleventh
Annual Convention of the American Manufacturers Export
Association, 14 October 1920, "Banking and Its Relationship to Domestic Business and Export Trade,
(pamphlet), p. 12.

[25]New York Times, 16 September 1920, p. 14.
Lamont spoke to a luncheon of the American Manufacturers
Export Association.

[26]Allan Walker, Manager of the Foreign Department
of the Guaranty Trust Company in a speech to the
American Manufacturers Export Association. New York

American trade with Asia, and with Latin America, compensated for the greater part of the loss in Europe. But the balance of trade worked against the United States and decreased the value of the dollar and the price of American goods. At the same time, a 200 per cent increase in the price of silver during 1918 and 1919 raised the purchasing power of Asia and India. But the post-war competition, and the decline in commodity and silver prices which began in Asia and Latin America late in 1919, precipitated a crash in the economies of these regions and lowered their imports from America. The value of American exports to Asia and the Western hemisphere dropped by more than 50 per cent in 1921.[27]

This sharp decline in commodity prices cut the value of some major American raw material imports by half, and American foreign banks involved in the production and financing of such crops as coffee, tea, and rubber, found themselves overextended. Many of the American branch banks in South America had to

---

Times, 22 April 1920, p. 21. A superficial summary of this development from the bankers' point of view may be found in the April 1920 issue of "The Americas," (a publication of the National City Bank), quoted in The Economic World, 1 May 1920, p. 619-622.

[27] Historical Statistics, p. 550.

close. So did some in Asia. The American Foreign
Banking Corporation, deeply involved in Cuban sugar
(and to some extent in Brazilian rubber) reduced its
capital from $58,500,000 to $20,000,000 in December
1920. The firm closed all but four of its 19 branches
in 1922, and a few years later sold the remaining
branches in Havana, Mexico City, Cristobal and Panama
City to the Chase National Bank.[28] The member banks
in the United States absorbed the slow Cuban accounts
(totalling about $8,000,000) in 1921.[29]

Similar difficulties befell the Mercantile Bank
of the Americas, one of the earliest American foreign
operations that had started extensive operations. The
Mercantile had become deeply involved in Colombian
coffee and Cuban sugar, for example; but, as in the
case of the American Foreign Banking Corporation, some
of its local officers proved less than trustworthy.
The Mercantile closed its European branches in Madrid,
Barcelona, and Hamburg, sold its Paris branch to the
Guaranty Trust Company, and transferred its Argentine

---

[28]NARS, RG59, 832.516/7, R. Mommsen, American
vice-consul in Rio de Janeiro, to Secretary of State
Lansing, 8 April 1918. Commercial and Financial
Chronicle, 25 December 1920, p. 2485.

[29]FRB, 421.27a, E. R. Kenzel (deputy-governor,
NYFRB) to Edmund S. Platt (vice-governor, Federal
Reserve Board), 20 May 1921.

branch to an American-Argentine syndicate.[30] Its
shareholding banks, predominantly Brown Brothers, and
J. W. Seligman and Company, extended $20,000,000 in
long-term funds to cover the over-extended operations
of the bank, and a syndicate headed by Morgan and
Company provided an additional $35,000,000 in credits
to help settle the bank's affairs. Eventually, the
remaining branches of the bank in Costa Rica, Nicaragua, Peru, Venezuela, and Colombia were reorganized
by a group of banks including the original stockholders,
and Morgan and Company, and the Guaranty Trust Company
into the Bank of Central and South America.[31]

The Park-Union Bank, which had doubled its
original $2,000,000 capital in 1920, concluded its Far
Eastern business in 1922 and merged with the successful

---

[30]FRB, 501.2, Daniel G. Mulloney (Chief National
Bank Examiner), to John Skelton Williams (Comptroller
of the United States), 24 October 1920. Commercial
and Financial Chronicle, 27 March 1920, p. 1243. New
York Times, 20 September 1921, p. 22. Ibid.,
9 February 1922, p. 24. Ibid., 13 August 1921,
p. 12.

[31]FRB, 421.27a, E. R. Kenzel (deputy Governor,
Federal Reserve Bank of New York) to Edmund S. Platt,
(vice-governor of the Federal Reserve Board), 20 May
1921. Also NARS, RG40, file 610, Eugene Stetson
(vice-president of the Guaranty Trust Company) to
Julius Klein (Bureau of Foreign and Domestic Commerce), 29 August 1921. New York Times, 10 June 1921,
p. 18. Ibid., 15 September 1922, p. 28.

Asia Banking Corporation, a Guaranty Trust institution.
The Asia Banking Corporation later sold its assets to
the International Banking Corporation, which was con-
trolled by the National City Bank.[32] But even National
City had to close eight of its 50 branches (in Colombia,
Capetown, Trinidad, and Brazil).[33]

While the total number of foreign branches declined after the contraction of 1921, the American
foreign banking system gained strength through the
concentration of authority in the hands of a relatively
smaller group of banks. Morgan and Company, the
Guaranty Trust, and the National City Bank (and to a
lesser extent, the Chase National Bank) became the
strongest--if not predominating influences--in American
foreign banking during the 1920's. But the contraction
in trade created uneasiness in view of widespread feeling in the United States that economic prosperity
depended on maintaining wartime markets. From 1914 to
1919, the increases in the capital invested in major
branches of manufacture had ranged from 25 per cent in
iron, steel, and textiles to 100 per cent in chemicals,

[32]New York Times, 15 March 1922, p. 27. Commercial and Financial Chronicle, 12 January 1924, p. 167-168.

[33]New York Times, 20 August 1921, p. 11. FRB,
421.2-24, /?/ (cashier National City Bank) to Walter
L. Eddy (assistant secretary Federal Reserve Board),
4 January 1922.

and 200 per cent in transportation equipment.[34] During
the same period, the export value of manufactured and
semi-manufactured goods increased by more than 300 per
cent.[35] The importance of farm exports to farm income
increased by about 75 per cent.[36] At the end of the
war, in 1919, exports composed 10 per cent of the gross
national product of the United States. That was an
increase of 66 per cent from 1914.[37] Such were the
figures behind the repeated remarks by bankers
describing foreign trade as the balance wheel of the
economy. The president of the National Bank of Commerce pointed out that a change of foreign trade
representing 5 per cent of the total could "mean a
loss of 20 to 40 per cent of the trade of some of our
important industries."[38] Another banker went so far
as to describe American foreign trade as the difference between a panic and boom on the domestic economy.[39]

[34]Historical Statistics, p. 411. See also "The
Stimulus of the War to American Manufactures as
Evidenced by the Foreign Trade," The Economic World,
9 February 1918, p. 193.

[35]Historical Statistics, p. 544.

[36]Historical Statistics, p. 542.

[37]Ibid.

[38]James S. Alexander, "Why We Must Have Foreign
Trade," 10 May 1922, (National Bank of Commerce:
pamphlet).

[39]Dr. Walter Lichtenstein (Foreign Trade Advisor

Yet other factors inherent in the domestic economy
worked to reduce that trade. The post-war demand for
capital and consumer goods (at home and abroad) created
enough pressure on the American economy to cause an
inflation in wholesale prices of about 22 per cent for
the 18 months from November 1918 to May 1920. Benjamin
Strong of the New York Federal Reserve Bank opposed
the inflation from the outset.[40] He felt the Federal
Reserve System could raise its rates and still compete
with England for the business of financing world
trade. His connections with English banking leaders
led him, in the summer of 1919, to conclude that the
British government would soon institute deflationary
policy. High bank rates would result, and Strong
judged that a good part of the English acceptance
business would then flow to New York if American deflation kept pace with the British. American problems of
post-war readjustment were so much less difficult than
those of any other nation, Strong wrote, "that in a

to the First National Bank of Chicago), Remarks to
Detroit Chapter of The American Institute of Banking,
14 December 1920, printed in Commercial and Financial
Chronicle, 15 January 1921, p. 211-212.

[40]NYFRB, file 790, Strong to Leffingwell, 22 November 1918. Leffingwell agreed in opposing inflation
but stipulated his desire that money rates remain
reasonable "to facilitate government financing without...causing speculation or credit expansion." See
Leffingwell to Bernard Baruch, NYFRB, file 790,
12 December 1918.

year or two we will be on the crest of the wave with the
world at our feet."

But he warned that continued inflation would defer
liquidation and prevent the establishment of lower
prices that were necessary to American postwar success.[41]
In April 1919, therefore, the Federal Reserve gave
serious consideration to raising the discount rate in
order to check the outflow of money from Reserve Bank
vaults, a notable result of the price rise.[42] The
Treasury Department also opposed the inflation but
resisted Strong's pressure for rate increases because
it believed that the postwar economy rendered the
Federal Reserve note control mechanisms useless. A rate
increase, according to Assistant Treasury Secretary
Leffingwell, would not producethe desired retarding
effect. It would simply increase the price of money,
curtail production, increase shortages, stimulate
speculation, and make inflation worse.[43] After the
failure of the Federal Reserve Board to take definite

[41]NYFRB, Strong Correspondence, Strong to Leffingwell, 6 February 1919. Also NYFRB, file 790, Strong to
Pierre Jay (chairman, NYFRB), 6 February 1919.

[42]Friedman and Schwartz, p. 222, quoting W. F. G.
Harding.

[43]NARS, RG56, Box 54, Federal Reserve Banks Discount Rate folder 1918-1920, policy memo of Leffingwell
for Carter Glass, 25 October 1919. By this time Leffingwell was definitely in favor of a rate increase.

steps against inflation, Strong and the New York Bank
favored a rate increase and tended to blame the continuing inflation, at least in part, on the growing
government debt fostered at a low rate of interest by
the Treasury.

The inflation continued and the Federal Reserve
Bank experienced a heavy outflow of gold after the lift-
ing of the embargo on that metal in June 1919. On his
tour of Europe that summer, Strong found further support for his preferred policies. In a conference with
G. Vissering of the Nederlandsche Bank, Strong agreed
that a policy of contraction might lead to a disaster
for the international economy, but that the banks should
work to check further expansion. Strong proposed cooperation based on a closer understanding between the
Bank of England, the Bank of France, Banque Nationale
de Belgique, the Nederlandsche Bank, the Federal Reserve Banks, and possibly the Reichsbank. Vissering
was "greatly interested."[44] Strong began to argue in
earnest for an increase in rates in September, and by
late October he had concluded that the reputation of
his Bank as a central banking institution depended upon
a rate increase.[45]

---

[44]NYFRB, Strong Diary, 8 August 1919.

[45]Friedman and Schwartz, p. 226.

The Treasury Department maintained its opposition to a rate increase. Leffingwell's view of the basic economic situation differed in three respects from Strong's. For one thing, the men occupied different positions in the system. As a Treasury official, Leffingwell was more reluctant than Strong to risk an increase in rates in government paper.[46] The second disagreement grew out of the Treasury's conclusion that the inflation was based on "crazy speculation," and the corollary that increases in the interest rate would not check it because the speculators were "figuring on short-term turnover and profits." Instead, the increases would "fall heavily on the legitimate borrower, who figured profits from industrial and commercial enterprise at a rate per annum."[47] Any increase in rates large enough to be effective would tend to curtail production at a time when, according to Leffingwell, the world was still short of goods. That would stimulate speculation because only the hope of great speculative profits would induce the borrower to transact any business on money borrowed at such high rates. Third, and probably most importantly, Leffingwell emphasized

---

[46]Leffingwell memo for Carter Glass, 25 October 1919, Carter Glass Papers, University of Virginia.

[47]Ibid.

(as Strong did not) an inevitable decline in American
foreign trade with Europe which, together with a
seasonal decline at the end of 1919 would cause a
liquidation, "with or without Federal Reserve Board
action."[48]

Leffingwell did not object to a rate increase,
"so arranged as not to embarrass the Treasury's plans."
He did feel that the Federal Reserve Board, as part of
such a rate increase, should insist that the Governors
of its banks exercise "a firm discrimination in making
loans and put an end to the abuse of the facilities of
the system in support of the reckless speculation in
stocks, land, cotton, clothing, foodstuffs and commodities generally."[49] Both Leffingwell and Secretary
Glass favored the perpetuation of the wartime Capital
Issues Committee during the reconversion period for
precisely the purpose of allocating capital on a pri-
ority basis.[50] Such forms of governmental control
could not flourish in the postwar political climate,

---

[48]Ibid., Leffingwell to W. P. G. Harding, 29 November 1919. Also Leffingwell memo re: Strong's letter
of 19 December 1919, memo dated 4 May 1920.

[49]Ibid.

[50]NARS, RG56, Capital Issues Committee file,
1918-1921, Carter Glass to C. S. Hamlin (Federal Reserve
Board), 3 January 1920. Warburg to Leffingwell,
4 February 1920, Warburg Papers, Yale University.
Leffingwell to Warburg, 11 February 1920, Warburg Papers,
Yale University.

however, when capital again went to the highest bidder.
Under those conditions, until production and saving
created a condition where the resources of the banks
met the requirements of their customers for commercial,
industrial, and governmental purposes, Leffingwell felt
that commercial rates would continue to be higher than
reserve bank rates. If reserve bank rates were increased, he argued, "a game of leapfrog will be played
between reserve bank rates and the government and commercial rates indefinitely until a prohibitive rate is
reached and business stops."[51]

Strong felt that Leffingwell's views ran counter
to the accepted doctrines of central banking. He
therefore opposed them. Strong particularly resisted
the idea that credit and currency would contract auto-
matically as trade demands diminished. "I would be
most regretful to learn," he wrote Leffingwell, "that
we differed on such a fundamental matter as this."[52]
In the second place, Strong denied that an increase in
the production of goods, "possibly coincident with a
reduction in our export trade," could be relied upon
to bring down prices and the volume of credit "without

[51]NARS, RG56, Box 54, Leffingwell memo for Glass,
25 October 1919.

[52]NYFRB, Strong Correspondence, Strong to Leffingwell, 8 October 1919.

any stimulation by rate changes."[53]   As a result of
that line of reasoning, Strong continued to work for a
rate increase.

An improvement in the position of the Treasury's
outstanding paper and, perhaps equally importantly,
the continuing inflation and outpouring of exports to
Europe during 1919, caused Secretary of Treasury Glass
to vote with the Federal Reserve Board for an increase
in rates in November and again in December.[54]   This did
not represent a change of basic Treasury policy.   On
the first occasion, Secretary Glass sent a letter
embodying Leffingwell's basic arguments to Board
Governor W. P. G. Harding with the plea that Harding
"not allow the Governors of the Federal Reserve Banks
to rely wholly or too heavily upon the increase in
rates."[55]

A bitter difference did develop between the New
York Federal Reserve Bank and the Treasury, but the
cause was not the question of commercial rates.   The
New York Bank unilaterally reduced rates on Treasury
certificates, while raising them on Liberty bonds,

----

[53]Ibid.

[54]Friedman and Schwartz, p. 227.

[55]NARS, RG56, Box 54, Federal Reserve Banks Discount Rate folder, Glass to W. P. G. Harding, 5 November
1919.

immediately after the Treasury had publicly announced
a new issue of Treasury certificates. At the same
time, the Bank proposed an increase in rate on commercial paper without taking the necessary preliminary
step of eliminating an existing arrangement with the
clearing house banks by which an increase in the rate
would have been accompanied by an automatic increase
in the rate for interbank deposits.[56] Glass, greatly
upset over the vast fiscal problems of reconversion,
felt that Strong's move was "menacing." He called the
Governor and his Board of Directors to Washington, "read
the riot act to the entire outfit," and vetoed the rate
changes.[57] At least one important director of the New
York Bank disassociated himself from the rate decrease
on Treasury certificates before this confrontation,
and Strong himself later said that his action was ill-
conceived and properly overruled by the Federal
Reserve Board.[58]

Strong nevertheless continued to blame the inflation on the natural desire of the Treasury to float its

[56]Ibid., Leffingwell memo re: Strong's letter of
19 December 1919, memo dated 5 May 1920.

[57]Carter Glass to Colonel Edward M. House,
13 December 1919, Carter Glass Papers, University of
Virginia.

[58]NARS, RG56, Leffingwell memo re: Strong's letter
of 19 December 1919, memo date 4 May 1920.

loans at low interest and to assert control over the
central bank "more distinctly in the interest of the
Treasury than in the interest of the general business
of the country."[59]   The Treasury, on the other hand,
took great pains to point out that its issues were not
inflationary.   Leffingwell claimed a "very gratifying,
normal and healthy absorption of these.../Treasury
notes_7 by the investing public," and blamed the inflation on bank credit for commercial purposes.   Strong
was elated when Glass agreed to another rate increase
in December 1919 which did not jeopardize Treasury
certificates.   Strong even felt that the Federal Reserve
System was on the verge of being "a real central bank,"
with all discounts approaching a uniform rate.[60]   Leffingwell summed up the controversy over rates in May
1920, concluding "there never was any really important
difference between Strong and me /Treasury Department_7
as to Reserve Bank rates."[61]

Strong had tried to preserve a preferential rate
on bankers acceptances because he wanted American
acceptances to play an important role in the international

---

[59]Strong to Leffingwell, 19 December 1919, Carter
Glass Papers, University of Virginia.

[60]Friedman and Schwartz, p. 227.

[61]NARS, RG56, Box 54, Leffingwell memo re: Strong's
letter of 19 December 1919, memo dated 4 May 1920.

economy, but also because he felt they were a better
asset than any other type of commercial paper. But
with the increase in commercial rates, acceptance bankers felt the pressure for available funds and they
appealed to the New York Federal Reserve Bank for an
increase in acceptance rates in order to raise their
own rates and compete for available funds. The Bank
reluctantly granted this increase on December 27, 1919,
raising the rate to 4 7/8% for 90-day bills. The same
afternoon, after the action became known, most dealers
raised their rates 1/8% above the Bank rate. Another
increase in January 1920 boosted the Bank discount rate
to 6%.[62]

The creation of credit by the banks through the use
of their acceptance powers continued to increase through
May 1920, when $673,852,000, the maximum acceptance
liability of member banks was reported. About three-
quarters of those acceptances originated in United
States foreign trade, with somewhat the larger portion
based on imports. To reduce this expansion, the
Federal Reserve Board had to reinforce the rate
structure of the System with quota restrictions. The
Board obtained legislation from the Congress that

---

[62]New York Times, 20 November 1919, p. 20. Commercial and Financial Chronicle, 22 November 1919,
p. 1934. Commercial and Financial Chronicle, 27 December 1919, p. 2401.

enabled it to control the amount of advances by any
Federal Reserve Bank to a specific borrowing bank.
That enabled the Board to reduce excessive borrowings
of member banks and force them to hold their own
borrowers in check without raising the basic discount
rate to moderate borrowers.[63] The proportion of
bankers' acceptances held by the Federal Reserve System
thereafter declined steadily from 55 per cent of the
total outstanding to about 19 per cent in April 1921.[64]

In spite of the Board's policy, New York member
banks maintained their acceptance liabilities on their
own responsibility, and Cleveland and Detroit member
banks refused to reduce acceptances. While the over-
all decline of acceptance liabilities proceeded rapidly,
those of the New York banks (in and out of the System)
showed only a slight reduction over the entire period.
They remained at $446 million a month through June
1921.[65] Acceptance liabilities of the member banks in
New York City constituted 61.9 per cent of the acceptance

---

[63]Federal Reserve Bulletin, May 1920, p. 448.
New York Times, 4 April 1920, p. 7. New York Times,
2 April 1920, p. 23. New York Times, 1 April 1920,
p. 19. New York Times (editorial), 23 May 1920,
Part II, p. 2.

[64]Federal Reserve Bulletin, July 1921, p. 776.

[65]Ibid., p. 776.

liabilities of all member banks in April 1921, as compared with 47 per cent in May 1920.[66]

As the flow of dollars abroad declined, the price
of dollars in relation to other foreign currencies
rose sharply. This caused hardships for foreign importers of American goods. Under such difficult conditions of exchange, the abnormal demands on American
foreign banking partially subsided. But exports continued to flow abroad and to Europe in record-breaking
quantity. Merchants and manufacturers, tempted by the
high prices they could obtain, continued to ship on
the basis of their own credit with the banks.[67] In
some cases, traders employed expedients which bypassed
the use of exchange altogether. European manufacturers,
for example, fabricated raw materials and then paid for
them by shipping a portion of the manufactured goods
back to the United States.[68]

American exporters also began to revive the practice of using sterling bills to finance their

---

[66]Ibid., p. 800.

[67]Eugene Meyer, Jr., address to the Industrial
Club of Chicago, 26 March 1920 (pamphlet), p. 8.
NARS, RG62, Frank B. Anderson (President, Bank of
California), to Commonwealth Club of California,
17 December 1920.

[68]Federal Reserve Bulletin, February 1920, p. 115.
Federal Reserve Bulletin, May 1920, p. 450.

transactions.[69] That expedient was short-lived, however, for the Bank of England and other central banks
of Europe (and Japan) raised their rates in recognition
of the necessity for controlling the prevailing demand
for credit. The advance of the London rate to a point
always above, and sometimes far above, the New York
rate during the period from April 1920 to March 1921
accounted in part for the marked increase in the amount
of dollar exchange created to finance trade between
countries other than the United States. The use of
these bills increased by 1000 per cent from December
1919 to May 1921, unmistakably revealing the confirma-
tion of dollar exchange by the international economy.[70]

Some sources interpreted the Bank of England rate
hike to 7% in April 1920 as an effort to force American
trade through New York rather than London.[71] Sir
Frederick Huth Jackson of the London acceptance house
of Frederick Huth & Company explained to officers of
the New York Federal Reserve Bank, however, that inflationary conditions similar to those prevailing in the
United States had compelled the Bank to make the
increase. Sir Frederick, chairman of the Association

[69]Chandler, Strong, p. 307.

[70]Federal Reserve Bulletin, September 1921, p. 1052.

[71]New York Times, 16 April 1920, p. 12.

of Accepting Bankers of the City of London, disclaimed
personal knowledge of any use of sterling bills by
American exporters or importers and hoped for none.[72]
He felt that the only hope for countries outside of the
United States (and England and its colonies) to obtain
required imports lay in the ability and willingness of
the United States to extend the necessary credits.
England could no longer meet that need. British
exports were then at 50 per cent of their pre-war
volume, yet Jackson expected them to decline further
because England could no longer finance its trade on
the former scale.[73] He was referring, for the most,
to long-term foreign investments; but there was little
doubt that he included the acceptance and discount
system because he had personally arranged a partnership
for his firm with a New York bank to transact dollar
business, particularly with the South American markets.[74]

The drop in commodity prices, the continued high
prices of American manufactured goods, the general
decline of international trade, and a highly competitive
$3\frac{1}{4}$% rate in London (compared to 4 1/8% in New York) all

[72]NYFRB, file 790, Memo of conversation between
E. R. Kenzel (NYFRB) and Sir Frederick Huth Jackson,
15 December 1920.

[73]Ibid.

[74]Ibid.

contributed to the decline in the volume of acceptances through 1921.[75] To save the system, the Federal Reserve Bank of New York worked for the liberalization of Federal Reserve Board regulations governing acceptances. It had some success. In May 1921, the Board allowed the rediscount by Federal Reserve Banks of acceptances to run from four to six months. Then, early in 1922, the Board conferred considerable discretionary power upon member banks in accepting bills for foreign trade, and upon the reserve banks for determining the eligibility of such bankers' acceptances. The purpose was "the general advancement of the foreign trade with the resulting benefit to agricultural and commercial interests which are largely dependent upon foreign markets."[76]

The position of acceptances was further enhanced by their use as a sound short-term investment by an increasing number of banks, business houses, and even individual investors. The executives of New York Life, Equitable Life, and other life insurance companies agitated for the reform of New York State law which

[75]NYFRB, file 440, letter from Bank to all Federal Reserve Banks, 7 March 1922.

[76]Paul Warburg, Federal Reserve System, Volume II, p. 820. W. P. G. Harding, "The Federal Reserve Banks and the Development of Bankers' Acceptances in the United States," quoted in The Economic World, p. 801. 10 June 1922. New York Times, 28 March 1922, p. 16.

prohibited insurance companies from investing in such
bills. Real estate interests in New York State lost a
fight in the legislature to prohibit savings banks
from investing in acceptances, and by the end of 1921
all but nine American states allowed savings banks to
put their money in this short-term form.[77] Perhaps
even more significantly, European investors began to
put large amounts into American dollar acceptances.
The American Acceptance Council estimated that foreign
institutions held about $300 million in American
acceptances in 1921 as a primary reserve for balances
kept for one reason or another in the United States.[78]

Another significant advance during this difficult
period came in the formation of the International
Acceptance Bank. It joined the foreign interests of
several important eastern banks with a group of Dutch,
Swiss, English, French, and Swedish banks. By working
directly through the extensive connections of the
European banks, particularly in Scandinavia and Central
Europe, funds of the First National Bank of Boston, the
American International Corporation, and other American
financial organizations were made available for

---

[77]Acceptance Bulletin, January 1922, p. 13. For
the use of acceptances by insurance companies see Ibid.,
January 1921, p. 5.

[78]New York Times, 30 September 1921, p. 21.

reputable trade financing at short-term. Foreign interests subscribed one-third of the capital stock of $10 million (with a surplus of $5 million). The movement of cotton, wheat, and other American products to Europe was financed largely through an acceptance syndicate. A number of banks participated in a given transaction, each being responsible for a specific amount and all protected through the hypothecation of collateral. The bank could finance about $150 million in yearly trade. Reports of the officers indicated steady profits and an annual dividend of about 8 per cent.[79]

Still another venture in acceptance banking was the First Federal Foreign Banking Association. That was underwritten by a group of eastern banks to help manufacturing interests (including the Savage Arms Company and the Baldwin Locomotive Works).[80] The First Federal, though an Edge Act Corporation entitled to finance trade with long-term securities, succeeded by operating almost exclusively as an acceptance bank during its first years. The banks and financial houses connected with

---

[79]Paul Warburg, Report No. 1 to Daniel Wing, 7 July 1920, Felix M. Warburg Collection, Box No. 194, P. M. Warburg folder, American Jewish Archives, Hebrew Union College. Ibid., Box 223, Reports of J. Abbott Goodhue (president of the Bank). New York Times, 14 February 1921, p. 18. Commercial and Financial Chronicle, 19 February 1921, p. 702.

[80]Commercial and Financial Chronicle, 24 April 1920, p. 1701-1702.

the manufacturing interests that were involved held the
entire subscription. Upon the formation of the Bank
in early 1920, William S. Kies, the Chairman of the
Board and former officer of the American International
Corporation, embarked for Europe to study the possibilities of granting credits.

Kies showed small interest in European securities.
He wanted sure markets for his clients and he saw
safety in acceptances rather than in long-term banking.
But he did try to persuade the Federal Reserve Board
to institute a change in its acceptance policy to allow
the creation of acceptances running one or two years.
That would enable the American manufacturer (or his
bank) to float notes to the investing public and then
carry outstanding balances abroad. Such long-term
acceptances would not have had re-discount privileges
at Federal Reserve Banks, and they would not necessarily
relate to any direct commercial transaction. The
Board's legal counsel discouraged the proposal on the
grounds that it might stimulate speculation with such
long-term acceptances on the basis of fluctuations in
foreign exchange rates.[81]

---

[81]FRB, 111.211, Kies to George Harrison (counsel
to the FRB), 31 March 1920. Ibid., Harrison to Kies,
2 April 1920.

Kies was not optimistic about extensive long-term
operations in Europe, and did not seriously consider
the possibility of debenture financing until 1923.[82]
He planned the operations of his bank in cooperation
with tested European banks that guaranteed repayment to
the First Federal. The Bank began business early in
1920 and charged about 6 1/8% for its accepting
services (including all commissions and discounts).
Under the Federal law it was permitted to incur obligations to 10 times its capital and surplus, or to
about $30 million. In its first full year of operation
it extended acceptances totaling $28.9 million, and
turned a net profit of $207,972.[83] The selective
strategy of Kies, which secured export trade for his
manufacturing clients and guaranteed repayment for his
bank, characterized the American export movement of
1921.

The same sharp demand for short-term capital that
persuaded the Federal Reserve Banks to raise their

[82]Kies to Vanderlip, 25 January 1924, Vanderlip
Papers, Columbia University.

[83]Commercial and Financial Chronicle, 2 October
1920, p. 1324. New York Times, 20 January 1922, p. 25.
A second Edge Act bank was set up in 1921 to finance
cotton exports. This was the Federal International
Banking Corporation. This bank and The First Federal
were liquidated after a few years of operation. Don
Woodland, "Financing Under the Edge Act," unpublished
dissertation, University of Texas, 1962.

discount rates affected the rates of long-term capital.
In the home market, the construction and railroad
industries made heavy demands on domestic credit, and
those calls, combined with the general shortage, forced
long-term rates upward.[84] Consequently, the Federal
Reserve discount policy designed to force exports
finance to turn to long-term credit from savings faced
considerable difficulties in practice. That was particularly true after the practical termination of United
States government aid to Europe in November 1919. As
part of the credit contraction policy, the Federal Reserve Board and the Treasury Department exercised their
influence in 1919 and 1920 to discourage new flotations
of stock unless the promoters could give reasonable
assurances that the issues would be sold to investors
and not ultimately lodged in the banks.[85] As the credit
restriction began to appear in 1920, large sales of
Liberty Bonds began to occur. The stock market dropped
in November and again in December. Especially hard hit
were the stocks of large corporations with overseas
interests.[86]

---

[84]_Federal Reserve Bulletin_, February 1920, p. 114.

[85]_Ibid_. Also _New York Times_, 3 February 1920, p. 22.

[86]_New York Times_, 19 May 1920, p. 1. _New York Times_, 20 November 1920, p. 1.

American bankers realized as early as 1919 that
the increasing domestic demand for credit would make it
difficult to market any great quantity of direct obligations of foreign governments, or debentures of the
proposed Edge Act corporations. The Guaranty Trust
Company, for example, encountered great resistance in
selling European bonds to American investors in 1919,
and attributed the trouble to the investors' exaggerated
fears over European conditions and to a general prefer-
ence for tax-exempt preferred stocks and government
bonds.[87] Such understanding helped to temper the
disappointment of those leaders in the financial district
who preferred to have the United States ratify the
Versailles Peace Treaty in November 1919, even though
the delay in formulating a European settlement promised to prolong European political and economic
instability, retard American investment there, and
reduce American exports.[88] Other Wall Street leaders,
however, were weary of the long fight over the treaty
and did not manifest so much concern over the defeat
of the League commitment.

---

[87]NARS, RG40, file 640, H. Stanley (vice president, Guaranty Trust Company) to Philip H. Kennedy
(director, bureau of foreign and domestic commerce),
29 August 1919.

[88]New York Times, 21 November 1919, p. 3.

The shortage of capital severely checked foreign
loans in the United States during 1919 and 1920, and
explains the failure (despite attractive interest
rates) of the attempt by the British Government to float
a $250 million issue, and the French effort to sell a
$45 million issue for cities in October 1919.[89] The
prospects for American involvement in South America
were also dim. The Treasury officer heading the
American delegation to the Second Pan-American Financial
Conference warned that meeting that financiers of Central and South America would have to learn that the
situation had changed radically from the time when the
United States began to look into foreign investment as
a possible outlet for its capital. The conference
itself was crisper than the more elaborate and formal
First Conference, at least according to Paul Warburg.
"We are getting more down to business," he wrote, "and
away from oratory; however, the trouble is that in view
of our congested market we cannot talk very much
business either."[90] The administration especially

[89]NARS, RG56, WFC, Leffingwell to T. W. Lamont,
18 November 1919 (item removed to Tax file, 18 November 1919). For details of the British Loan see New
York Times, 26 October 1919, p. 23.

[90]NYFRB, Strong Correspondence, Warburg to
Strong, 26 January 1920. For the Treasury Department
view of the Conference and financial problems see
NARS, RG56, C. E. McGuire, memo and confidential report
for Assistant Secretary Rowe, 10 March 1920.

discouraged loans to South American nations which (like
Argentina) enjoyed a favorable balance of trade with
the United States. Such loans would only increase the
outflow of gold from the United States, and that was
against the policies of the Federal Reserve Board and
the Treasury Department. Norman Davis of the Treasury
concluded that "we cannot expect to continue to finance
our debtors in Europe and our creditors in South
America."[91]

The United States was also failing Europe. The
net outflow of assistance from the United States
Government dropped $2,153 million in 1920, and net
private capital outflow increased only $554 million.
The British could not offer much assistance in Europe,
although their government was prepared to launch a
powerful export drive to the continent with £26,000,000
in loans to private interests. The program failed
because British exporters, like their American counterparts, were reluctant to move into the unstable business
climate in Europe. The Chancellor of the Exchequer
explained the situation to Leffingwell. "I have little
confidence that there are potential borrowers
sufficiently solvent to justify the receipt of such

---

[91]NARS, RG39, Country files, Box 203, Leffingwell
memo for Glass, 15 January 1920.

large advances."[92] The British government therefore
appealed to the credit resources of the United States.

To give Continental Europe a chance to stabilize,
and thereby enable Great Britain and the United States
to justify extending large credits, the Chancellor
strongly urged the Treasury to cancel the intergovernmental war debts.[93] The Treasury Department,
under the new leadership of Secretary David Houston,
expressed a willingness to discuss the funding of the
wartime governmental debts; but Houston argued that the
cancellation of the debts would not touch the causes
of the great European inflation, which he felt was the
cause of Europe's financial and economic difficulties.
"The relief of present ills," said Houston, "insofar
as it can be obtained, is primarily within the control
of the debtor governments and peoples themselves.
Most of the debtor governments have not levied taxes
sufficient to enable them to balance their budgets
nor have they taken any energetic and adequate measures
to reduce their expenditures."[94] Too little progress
had been made in deflating excessive issues of currency,

---

[92]NARS, RG59, 811.51/2500, Davis, Folk, and Leffingwell to Albert Rathbone, 5 March 1920, quotes Chancellor
of the Exchequer message to Leffingwell.

[93]Ibid.

[94]Ibid.

or in stabilizing the currencies at new levels. To the
contrary, in Continental Europe there had been a constant increase in note issues and, particularly, there
had been little effort to make reparations settlements
that would allow Germany and Austria to make their full
contribution to the economy of the Continent. Houston's
views represented, of course, a continuation of the
policy laid down by Glass and Leffingwell late in 1918.

In spite of what was in many respects an adverse
economic climate, the downward trend in American long-
term capital investments abroad reversed itself in 1920
and continued to improve during most of the next
decade.[95] The high surplus in international accounts
continued to decline and the increased investments,
particularly of the portfolio type, together with
unilateral remittances from nationality groups in the
United States, and sizable imports of gold, met the
requirements of the balance of trade. Those methods
of finance did not offset the sharp drop in government
aid, or the decline in enthusiasm of American manufacturers and exporters in 1919 and early 1920.
American foreign trade continued to decline in 1921
and thereafter hovered around 1913 levels both in
quantity and value.

---

[95]Historical Statistics, p. 564.

The earnest desire of some American manufacturers
for foreign markets, and the devaluation of foreign
currencies, offered foreign assets and commodities at
bargain prices for purchasers with dollars to spend.
Large corporations took most advantage of the resulting
attractive opportunities for direct investments. The
expansionist psychology of American business during the
1920's, and the resulting pressure for foreign markets
and assured sources of supply, stimulated the use of
funds from undistributed earnings to finance these
foreign ventures.[96]

The movement began shortly after the end of the
war when American corporations began to secure effective
control of established European corporations. The
great depreciation of the Austrian crown offered an
unusual opportunity that attracted capital from many
nations to the industrial and banking operations of
that nation. Kuhn, Loeb and Company, and the
Guaranty Trust Company, acquired an important interest
in the Viena Creditanstalt, the leading industrial and
commercial bank in the states which had comprised the
Austro-Hungarian empire. The bank had branches

[96]Hal B. Lary, The United States in the World
Economy (Washington; U.S.G.P.O., 1943), p. 102-3.
Commercial and Financial Chronicle, 19 March 1921,
p. 1086. FRC, Box 195, A. S. Strauss (Treasury)
memo for Russell Leffingwell.

throughout the old empire and in several cities of the
new Balkan states, and the move contributed to the
development of trade between the United States and
Southeastern Europe.[97] W. Averill Harriman and Company
acquired the Hamburg-American line and its modern ship-
yards, a venture that promised to make the Harriman
interests the largest shipping interests in the world.[98]
The American electrical and rubber industries established close working arrangements with their German
counterparts.[99] American interests also invested very
heavily in German real estate and hotels, which seemed
especially promising in view of the exchange differential.

The foundation of an American exchange for foreign
securities further encouraged the increase in American
foreign investment. Many bankers strongly advocated
this development as a means of financing the American
export trade and assisting in the reconstruction of
Europe. For lack of anything to sell immediately after
the war, European buyers offered collateral in the

---

[97]New York Times, 18 June 1920, p. 20. Federal
Reserve Bulletin, August 1920, p. 777. New York
Times, 14 December 1919, p. 7.

[98]New York Times, 6 June 1920, Section II, p. 1.

[99]Federal Reserve Bulletin, August 1920, p. 777.
New York Times, 9 May 1920, p. 2.

form of securities representing their assets. American
exporters would more readily accept these securities as
suitable and desirable collateral for goods if a
flourishing market made them readily negotiable for
cash.[100] Eugene Meyer of the War Finance Corporation
was especially energetic in urging the New York Stock
Exchange to list foreign securities. Most financial
interests favored the plan, but "a few relatively minor
banking houses" opposed it because they could sell
securities at a greater profit without an open market.
The biggest firm that opposed the idea was Morgan and
Company; it argued that the exchange risks were too
great for the public at large to comprehend.[101] But
Leffingwell tried to dissuade Lamont of that negative
view: "I am very anxious to convince you you are
wrong about this...you cannot deal with a great world
situation like this on the basis of obscuranticism."[102]

The New York Stock Exchange was opened to foreign
listings in 1921 after rules designed to cope with the
peculiarities of foreign paper had been adopted. Most

---

[100]FRC, RG39, World War I records, Box 95, Bonds
of Foreign Governments folder, Eugene Meyer, Jr., memo
for Secretary of Treasury Glass, 17 December 1919.
According to Meyer, General Electric thought the list-
ing for foreign loans on the Exchange would be
advantageous.

[101]Ibid., Leffingwell to Lamont, 18 December 1919.

[102]Ibid.

important was the decision to quote foreign paper on
the basis of a fixed rate of exchange, for that allowed
the fluctuations in exchange and the fluctuations in
value of the securities to be reflected in the market
price.[103] A comparison of the financial columns of
leading American newspapers with the metropolitan
dailies of Europe indicated that a comparatively small
number of foreign stocks and other securities were
reported in the press.[104] The American market lacked
the variety of the European market because the American
investing public lacked an extensive awareness of overseas operations.

Foreign bond and stock sales mounted sharply in
1922, spurred by the world-wide increase in railroad,
highway, and hydroelectric construction projects. A
record total of $92,300,000 in loans were issued by the
United States in January 1922, and the total continued
to climb: $155,500,000 in March; and $203,000,000 in
April.[105] South American nations, as well as Far
Eastern and European countries, participated in the
heavy borrowing. The massive loan program that was

---

[103]New York Times, 26 May 1921, p. 23.

[104]Notz and Harvey, American Foreign Trade (Indianapolis: Bobbs-Merrill Company, 1921), p. 323.

[105]Acceptance Bulletin, April 1922, p. 6.

anticipated as a result of the reorganization of the
Chinese consortium did not develop because of excessive
demands by the Americans, but the Continental and Commercial Trust and Savings Bank of Chicago agreed to
refund its earlier loan of $5,500,000 and extend an
additional $30,000,000.[106] In 1921 and 1922 Americans
took advantage of the British tendency to confine their
capital exports to Commonwealth nations and made the
first significant American loans to Asian nations. A
$100,000,000 issue of the Dutch East Indies was of
particular importance in demonstrating American financial power in the Far East.[107] The United States
loaned South America $230 million in 1921 and
$224,000,000 in 1922. While members of the American
group that had established connections in Latin
America before the war claimed preferential treatment,
sharp competition among American banks, and between
American banks and those of other nations, was the
rule in South America.[108]

---

[106]New York Times, 27 November 1921, p. 23. Ibid.,
9 November 1921, p. 14. United States Foreign Relations,
1921, Volume I, 893.51/3329, J. P. Morgan and Company
to Secretary of State Charles E. Hughes, 10 March
1921. New York Times, 24 November 1921, p. 19.

[107]Lary, op. cit., p. 94.

[108]New York Times, 16 February 1921, p. 19.
NARS, RG59, 833.51/170, P. S. Smith (chief Latin American

The years immediately following World War I
revealed that the United States had made a strong and
enduring financial commitment to the international
economy. In spite of its rapid and unstable growth
during the war years, the American discount and
acceptance system withstood the sharp contraction of
world trade in 1920. The attitude of British acceptance bankers and the striking increase in the use of
dollar exchange to finance trade between countries
other than the United States indicated that the
Americans had won a lasting role in the system of
international finance. Though the number of American
branch banks overseas declined from 181 in 1920 to
107 in 1926 to meet the postwar decline in international commerce, the American foreign banking system
remained potent by any standards.[109]

The bankers' efforts in the field of long-term
finance leaves little doubt that during the war years
American finance had moved into the world to stay.
The bankers fought to enlist the government's aid for
reconstruction and they succeeded to the extent of
winning the Edge Act and the extension of the War

Division bureau of foreign and domestic commerce, to
/?_7 Carrell (Latin American Division, State Department), 28 November 1921.

[109]Phelps, op. cit., pp. 131-132.

Finance Corporation. The government's basic determination to withdraw from the business of financing
American trade on a long-term, institutional basis,
forced the capital available for that task into a
highly competitive bidding situation created by the
demands of a booming domestic economy. The resulting
rising interest rates, exchange problems, and re-
strictive tariffs in Europe all played a part in
reducing American foreign business. Nevertheless,
American long-term loans abroad (of the direct and
portfolio types) increased fairly steadily from 1920
until the crash of 1929.

Chapter VII

Conclusion

The expansion of the American foreign banking
system rested on two motives that were basic to the
leaders of the American economy: 1) the concern of
the banking community to open a new field of profitable
operations, and 2) the desire of the commercial community and the government to continue and expand
American trade abroad. The impracticality of further
American financial dependence on Europe also played
an important part in motivating the American groups to
action. By accentuating this impracticality, World
War I greatly accelerated the growth of the American
foreign banking system.

The war disrupted patterns of world trade, and
produced great pressure for the growth of dollar exchange. Specifically, it reduced the importance of
sterling and opened the way for dollar exchange to play
an important role in the trade of South America and
Asia. Furthermore, the war required large amounts of
dollar exchange to finance the trade between the United
States and the Allied governments of Europe.

These effects caused the very rapid growth of
American acceptance liabilities and the development of
dollar exchange as a tool of American trade expansion.
This growth was distorted, however, by the pressure and
instability of wartime conditions. A large proportion
of acceptances created during the war years (the renewal credits) were banking transactions rather than
business arrangements arising from commercial deals.
The banking community revealed a disinterest in investing in discounting acceptances. The initial lack of
discount banks emphasized that negative attitude and
forced the American system to depend on the Federal
Reserve Banks.

But the world importance of the dollar exchange
prompted leading American bankers and banking institutions to support the dollar system, and to encourage
the banking and business community in the use of dollar
acceptances for commercial transactions by establishing
discount banks and encouraging the investment of short-
term funds in dollar acceptances. By 1920, those
efforts had secured the foundations of the American
acceptance and discount banking system. Summarizing
this stage of growth, it can be said that the war
unquestionably established the importance of the
American acceptance system and dollar exchange by

diminishing the influence of sterling and by increasing American exports.

The war likewise placed long-term lending in a new perspective by immensely increasing America's favorable balance of trade with Europe, and by shifting the dependence on long-term borrowing of the world's developing nations from the European belligerents to the United States. Neither of those developments had any uniquely significant effects on American foreign economic policy, but they did increase the country's international financial commitment and shaped the outlook of business and government leaders.

A major facet of this development was the financial community's expectation of a large and permanent increase in long-term capital investments abroad. This expectation intensified the bankers' interest in the problems connected with the export of finance capital, and in the question of proper protection by the government. The policies of the Wilson government towards the Chinese consortium, the Mexican Revolution, the promotion of close economic ties with South America, and of the investment bankers in the formation of the Foreign Securities Committee, reveal a strong predisposition (continuing from the Taft administration) for business and government to cooperate closely in formulating mutually satisfactory foreign economic policies involving the protection of American interests abroad.

The unique contribution of the war experience to this relationship came not from this more or less traditional type of government activity but from the decision to make massive loans to the Allied belligerents. This policy, which seemed natural enough during the period of American co-belligerency with the Allies, raised no dissent of any importance from leaders of finance or government. But the bankers and the government split over the issue of continuing such loans in peace time. By refusing to go on with the practice, the government eliminated itself from expensive and entangling financial relationships for which, it assumed, the electorate would not stand. The bankers, on the other hand, explicitly sought to continue the government's activities as a sponsor and participant in reconstruction. They wanted to popularize that kind of financial venture with the investing public and <u>reduce the financial risk</u> to themselves.

The consequences of the government decision to withdraw from direct aid seemed so grave to the bankers (and closely allied business interests) that they made prolonged efforts to institutionalize government financial support as part of the traditional

business-governmental alliance. Their argument for the
policy was partly humanitarian; but it was predominately
practical, growing out of the new perspective from
which the bankers viewed the world.

With the government's help, the bankers supervised
the nation's financial adjustments to its new place in
the international economy. The bankers had assumed
real and prospective global responsibilities which,
under crucial postwar conditions, they believed implied
new and lasting responsibilities for the government as
well. Specifically, they felt the new situation involved
the government in new financial responsibilities in
addition to the traditional diplomatic protection of
high-risk foreign markets.

The bankers lost the fight for government participation in European reconstruction, but they did
succeed in convincing the government that it had new
responsibilities implied by the American place in the
international economy. Due to the efforts of the
financial community, the government incorporated Edge
Act banks (and intended to encourage their operations
with government funds from the War Finance Corporation), and extended the War Finance Corporation
activities through the immediate postwar years as a
government subsidized high-risk export bank. The
work of the bankers greatly impressed business and

government leaders and pointed the way toward the more
direct involvement of the government in providing
capital that came during the decade of the 1930's.

APPENDIX

Balance of Payments Data, 1881-1957

Series U 168-192. Balance of International Payments: 1790 to 1957—Con.

[In millions of dollars]

Year	Balance on goods and services	Unilateral transfers, net [to foreign countries (-)] — Private	Government	U.S. capital, net [outflow of funds (-)] — Government, long- and short-term	Private — Direct[2]	Other long-term	Short-term	Foreign capital, net [outflow of funds (-)] — Long-term	Short-term	Changes in monetary gold stock [increase(-)]	Errors and omissions[3]
	182	183	184	185	186	187	188	189	190	191	192
1957	8,245	-543	-4,210	-958	-2,058	-859	-258	309	382	-798	+748
1956	6,455	-530	-4,447	-625	-1,859	-603	-528	395	1,409	-306	+643
1955	4,391	-444	-4,367	-310	-779	-241	-191	875	579	41	+446
1954	5,022	-486	-4,937	-98	-664	-320	-635	252	1,210	-298	+167
1953	4,691	-476	-6,491	-218	-721	-185	-667	124	1,023	1,161	+296
1952	4,948	-417	-6,691	-420	-850	-214	-94	443	1,169	-379	+505
1951	5,191	-386	-4,576	-156	-528	-437	-103	-477	1,055	-53	+470
1950	2,329	-444	-4,089	-156	-621	-495	-149	994	918	1,743	-30
1949	6,359	-521	-5,316	-652	-660	-80	187	119	-47	-164	+775
1948	6,740	-683	-4,128	-1,024	-721	-69	-116	-172	524	-1,530	+1,179
1947	11,572	-669	-1,986	-6,969	-749	-49	-189	-98	363	-2,162	+936
1946	7,813	-650	-2,318	-3,024	-230	127	-310	-347	-633	-623	+195
1945	6,041	-473	-6,640	-1,019	-100	-354	-96	-104	2,189	548	+8
1944	12,452	-357	-13,785	-231	71	-62	-85	175	509	1,350	-37
1943	11,038	-249	-12,658	-109	98	-58	-12	-84	1,222	757	+34
1942	6,413	-122	-6,213	-221	19	-84	96	-327	182	23	-8
1941	2,410	-179	-957	-391	47	19	21		-400	-719	+476
1940	1,719	-178	-82	-51	32	36	177	-90	1,353	-4,243	+1,277
1939	1,066	-151	-27	14	9	104	226	-86	1,259	-3,174	-788
1938	1,148	-153	-29	-9	16	24	36	57	317	-1,794	+249
1937	1,291	-217	-21	-2	35	241	43	245	311	-1,364	+425
1936	115	-176	-32	3	-12	189	52	600	376	-1,272	+157
1935	128	-162	-20	-5	34	82	427	320	648	-1,822	-364
1934	601	-162	-10	-7	-17	202	104	9 915	126	-1,266	+412
1933	358	-191	-17	2	32	-80	42	125	-454	131	+61
1932	407	-217	-21	26	-16	267	227	-26	-673	-53	+79
1931	516	-279	-40	14	-222	350	628	66	-1,265	133	+99
1930	1,032	-306	-36	77	-294	-70	-191	66	-288	-310	-320
1929	1,148	-343	-34	38	-602	-34	-200	358	196	-143	-384
1928	1,377	-346	-19	49	-558	-752	-231	463	-117	238	-104
1927	1,073	-355	-2	46	-351	-636	-349	-50	934	113	-423
1926	826	-361	-20	30	-351	-470	-36	95	455	-93	-75
1925	1,087	-373	-30	27	-268	-603	-46	10 301	-60	100	-135
1924	1,351	-389	-25	28	-182	-703	-109	10 185	228	-256	-178
1923	842	-328	-37	91	-148	-235	-82	10 338	49	-315	-175
1922	997	-314	-38	91	-153	-669		-4		-269	+408
1921	2,122	-450	-59	30	-111	-477				-735	-316
1920	3,523	-684	-45	-175	-154	-400		-278	422	68	-1,905
1919	4,868	-832	-212	-2,328	-94	-75		-215	400	166	-1,278
1918	2,458	-268		-4,028		-396			-900	-5	1,817
1917	3,475	-180	-25	-3,656		-594		-36		-312	+928
1916	3,102	-150				-1,064		-391		-531	-66
1915	1,748	-150		-76		-790		-789	450	-499	+30
1914	56	-170		-188		-14		432	450	100	+86
1913	374	-207		-189		-27		252		-25	-229
1912	257	-212		-95		-70		232		-81	+13
1911	274	-224				-28		171		-90	-8
1910	46	-204			-124	34		345		-71	-26
1909	26	-187			-88	-24		171		18	+84
1908	427	-192			-48	-87		89		-44	-145
1907	296	-296			-89	24		136		-154	-36
1906	296	-147			-92	46		114		-171	-46
1905	298	-133	-10	-40	-46	-93		56		-71	-11
1904	279	-127			-80	11		59		-25	-67
1903	340	-115			-81	40		20		-71	-133
1902	258	-105			-65	-40		-30		-71	-53
1901	438	-104			-89	-123		-33		-61	-28
1900 [4]	507	-95	-20		-56	87	-296	-75		-91	-103
1899	429	-54					-279			-78	
1898	427	-48					-279			-130	
1897	444	-44					-23			-121	
1896	132	-41					-40			-68	
1895	-127	-55					137			44	11
1894	98	-54					-66			22	
1893	-119	-44					146			17	
1892	-20	-50					41			33	
1891	-90						136			4	
1890	-150	-45					194			1	
1889	-166	-44					202			8	
1888	-226	-30					287			-30	
1887	-157	-28					231			-46	
1886	-77	-28					137			-32	
1885	12	-27					34			-19	
1884	-59	-24					105			-23	
1883	-12	-22					51			-17	
1882	-55	-13					110			-42	
1881	137	-5					-41			-91	

BIBLIOGRAPHY

I. Government Publications

United States. Bureau of the Census. <u>Historical Statis-</u>
<u>tics of the United States, Colonial Times to</u>
<u>1957</u>. Washington, 1960.

_____. Federal Trade Commission. <u>Report on Co-</u>
<u>operation in American Export Trade</u>. Part I.
Summary and Report. Washington, 1916.

_____. Department of Commerce. Lary, Hal B. and
Associates. <u>The United States in the World</u>
<u>Economy</u>. Washington, 1943.

_____. Department of Commerce. Bureau of Foreign
and Domestic Commerce. Special Agents Series.
No. 106. Lough, William H. <u>Banking Oppor-</u>
<u>tunities in South America</u>. Washington, 1905.

_____. Department of Commerce. Bureau of Foreign
and Domestic Commerce. Special Agents Series.
No. 62. Wolfe, Archibald J. <u>Foreign Credits</u>.
Washington, 1913.

_____. Department of Commerce. Special Agents
Series. No. 90. Senate Document No. 659. 63rd
Congress, 3rd Session. <u>Banking and Credit in</u>
<u>Argentina, Brazil, and Chile</u>. Washington, 1914.

United States Senate. 62nd Congress, 2nd Session.
Document No. 243. <u>The National Monetary Com-</u>
<u>mission Report</u>. Washington, 1912.

_____. 63rd Congress, 1st Session. Document No. 232.
<u>Hearings of the Banking and Currency Committee</u>
<u>on a Bill to Establish Federal Reserve Banks</u>.
Washington, 1913.

_____. 63rd Congress, 3rd Session. Document No.
714. <u>Report of the Latin American Trade Com-</u>
<u>mittee</u>. Washington, 1915.

_____. 65th Congress, 2nd Session. <u>Hearings Before</u>
<u>the Committee on Banking and Currency on the</u>
<u>Federal Reserve Foreign Bank</u>. Washington, 1918.

_____. 67th Congress, 2nd Session. Document No. 86.
<u>Loans to Foreign Governments</u>. Washington, 1921.

_____. 74th Congress, 2nd Session. Hearings of the Special Committee Investigating the Munitions Industry. Washington, 1936.

United States House of Representatives. 65th Congress, 3rd Session. Hearings of the Committee on Finance on the Fifth Liberty Bond Bill. Washington, 1919.

_____. 62nd Congress, 3rd Session. Hearings of the Subcommittee of the Committee on Banking and Currency Investigating the Money Trust. Washington, 1913.

_____. 66th Congress, 3rd Session. Hearings Before the Committee on Banking and Currency on the War Finance Corporation. Washington, 1920.

_____. 66th Congress, /no session specified7. Hearings Before the Committee on Banking and Currency on S. 2472 to amend the Federal Reserve Act.

United States Library of Congress. Selected List of Books with References to Periodicals Relating to Currency and Banking with Special Regard to Recent Conditions. Washington, 1908.

_____. Special List of References on the Monetary Question. Compiled by Herman H. B. Meyer and William Adams Slade. Washington, 1908.

II. Manuscript Collections

Bernard Baruch Papers, Princeton University Library.

Board of Governors of the Federal Reserve System, Washington, D. C.

Bainbridge Colby Papers, Library of Congress.

Commerce Department Records, National Archives.

Norman H. Davis Papers, Library of Congress.

Carter Glass Papers, University of Virginia.

Charles Hamlin Papers, Library of Congress.

Edwin N. Hurley Papers, Notre Dame University.

Fred I. Kent Papers, Princeton.

Breckenridge Long Papers, Library of Congress.

Franklin Mac Veagh Papers, Library of Congress.

William Gibbs McAdoo Papers, Library of Congress.

New York Federal Reserve Bank Records, New York Federal
    Reserve Bank.

Frank Polk Papers, Library of Congress.

Elihu Root Papers, Library of Congress.

State Department Records, National Archives.

Treasury Department Records, National Archives.

Treasury Department Records, Federal Records Center,
    Arlington, Virginia

Frank Vanderlip Papers, Columbia University.

Paul M. Warburg Papers, Yale University.

III. Newspapers and Periodicals

Acceptance Bulletin, 1916-1922.

American Exporter, various issues.

Americas, various issues.

Asia, various issues.

Bankers' Magazine, 1907-1921.

Commercial and Financial Chronicle, 1907-1921.

Economic World, 1915-1922.

Federal Reserve Board Annual Report, 1915-1922.

Federal Reserve Bulletin, 1915-1922.

Journal of the American Bankers' Association,
        1907-1922.

Journal of the Institute of Bankers, various issues.

Journal of the Investment Bankers Association of
        America, 1911-1924.

London Economist, various issues.

London Times, 1907-1915.

New York Times, 1907-1921.

World's Markets, 1907-1921.

IV. Pamphlets

James S. Alexander. Address to the Eleventh Annual
        Convention of the American Manufacturers Export
        Association. 14 October 1920. "Banking and
        Its Relationship to Domestic Business and
        Export Trade."

_____. "Why We Must Have Foreign Trade." Address
        at the Ninth National Foreign Trade Council.
        May 10, 1922. National Bank of Commerce, New
        York.

W. S. Kies. "Bank Expansion through Foreign Branches
        under the Federal Reserve Bank." National
        City Bank, New York, 1916.

V. Unpublished Dissertations and Theses

Don Woodland. "Financing Under the Edge Act."
        Doctoral Dissertation. University of Texas,
        1962.

Matthew Simon. "Cyclical Fluctuations and the Inter-
        national Capital Movements of the United States,
        1865-1897." Doctoral Dissertation. Columbia
        University, 1955.

Martin J. Sklar. "Woodrow Wilson, The Six-Power
        Consortium and Dollar Diplomacy." Masters
        Thesis. University of Wisconsin, 1962.

VI. Books

Angell, James W. <u>Financial Foreign Policy of the</u>
    <u>United States</u>. New York: Russell & Russell,
    1965.

Beckhart, Benjamin. <u>Discount Policy of the Federal</u>
    <u>Reserve System</u>. New York: Henry Holt and
    Company, 1924.

Brown, John Crosby. <u>A Hundred Years of Merchant Bank-</u>
    <u>ing</u>. New York: Privately Printed, 1909.

Campbell, Charles S., Jr. <u>Special Business Interests</u>
    <u>and the Open Door Policy</u>. New Haven: Yale
    University Press, 1951.

Chandler, Lester V. <u>Benjamin Strong, Central Banker</u>.
    The Brookings Institution. Washington, D. C.,
    1958.

Croly, Herbert. <u>Willard Straight</u>. New York: MacMillan
    Company, 1925.

Edwards, George W. <u>Investing in Foreign Securities</u>.
    New York: The Ronald Press, 1926.

Fayle, C. Ernest. <u>A Short History of the World's</u>
    <u>Shipping Industry</u>. London: George Allen and
    Unwin Ltd., 1933.

Feis, Herbert. <u>The Diplomacy of the Dollar</u>. Balti-
    more: John Hopkins Press, 1950.

Haight, Frank Arnold. <u>A History of French Commer-</u>
    <u>cial Policies</u>. New York: MacMillan Company,
    1941.

Hirst, Francis W. <u>The Consequences of the War to Great</u>
    <u>Britain, Economic and Social History of the</u>
    <u>World War</u>. British Series. London: Humphrey
    Milford Oxford University Press, New Haven:
    Yale University Press, 1934.

Hough, B. Olney. <u>Elementary Lessons in Exporting</u>.
    New York: Johnson Export Publishing Company,
    1909.

_____. Practical Exporting. 3rd Edition Revised. New York: Johnson Export Publishing Company, 1919.

Houston, David F. Eight Years with Wilson's Cabinet. 1913-1920. Two volumes. New York, 1926.

James, F. Cyril. The Growth of Chicago Banks. Volume 1. New York: Harper Brothers, 1938.

Josepheson, Matthew. The President Makers. 1896-1919. New York, 1940.

King, W. T. C. A History of the London Discount Market. George Rutledge & Sons, Ltd., 1936.

Laughlin, J. Lawrence (ed.). Banking Reform. Chicago: The National Citizens League, 1912.

Monetary Commission. Report of the Monetary Commission of the Indianapolis Monetary Convention. Chicago: University of Chicago Press, 1898.

Notz and Harvey. American Foreign Trade. Indianapolis: Bobbs-Merrill Company, 1921.

Noyes, Alexander D. Forty Years of American Finance. New York: G. P. Putnam's Sons, 1898.

_____. The War Period of American Finance. New York, 1926.

Phelps, Clyde W. The Foreign Expansion of American Banks. New York: Ronald Press, 1927.

National Association of Manufacturers. Proceedings of the International Trade Conference. New York, 1915.

Schluter, William C. The Pre-War Business Cycle, 1907-1914. Published Dissertation of Columbia University, 1923.

Stephenson, Nathaniel W. Nelson W. Aldrich. New York:
    D. Apellton Century Company, 1935.

Tillman, Seth P. Anglo-American Relations of the Paris
    Peace Conference of 1919. Princeton: Prince-
    ton University Press, 1961.

Tippetts, Charles S., Jr. State Banks and the Federal
    Reserve System. New York: D. Van Nostrand
    Company, Inc., 1929.

Turlington, Edgar. Mexico and Her Foreign Creditors.
    New York: Columbia University Press, 1930.

Vanderlip, Frank. What Happened to Europe. New York:
    MacMillan Company, 1919.

_____. From Farm Boy to Financier. New York:
    D. Apellton Century Company, 1935.

Wainwright, Nicholas B. History of the Philadelphia
    National Bank. Philadelphia: Philadelphia
    National Bank, 1953.

Warburg, Paul M. The Federal Reserve System. Two
    Volumes. New York: The MacMillan Company,
    1930.

Ward, Willard. Bank Credits and Acceptances. New
    York: The Ronald Press, 1931.

Williams, John H. Argentine International Trade under
    Inconvertible Paper Money, 1880-1900.
    Cambridge: Harvard University Press, 1920.

Willoughby, Woodbury. The Capital Issues Committee
    and the War Finance Corporation, The John
    Hopkins University Studies in Historical and
    Political Science. Volume 52. Baltimore:
    John Hopkins, 1924.

Yamasaki, Kukujiro, and Ogawa, Gotar. Effect of the
    War on the Commerce and Industry of Japan,
    Economic and Social History of the World War.
    New Haven: Yale University Press, 1929.

VII. Articles

Cole, Arthur H. "Evolution of the Foreign Exchange
        Market of the United States." Journal of
        Business and Economic History. May 1929.

Downs, William C. "The Commission House in Latin
        American Trade." Quarterly Journal of Eco-
        nomics. November 1911.

Mantoux, Paul. "Trade with France Before and After
        the War." Journal of the Royal Statistical
        Society. May 1917.

Owens, Richard N. "The Hundred Million Dollar Foreign
        Trade Financing Corporation." Journal of
        Political Economy. January 1922.

Reynolds, George. "The Effect of the European War on
        American Credits." Journal of Political
        Economy. Volume 22.

Smith, Robert F. "The Formation and Development of
        the International Bankers Committee on
        Mexico." Journal of Economic History.
        December 1963.

_____. "Thomas W. Lamont and United States -
        Mexican Relations." Harvard Library Bulletin.
        January 1967.

Strait, Willard. "China's Loan Negotiations." Journal
        of Race Development. Volume 3, April 1913.

Taussig, Frank W. "The Difficulties of the Country's
        Tariff Problems Under Existing International
        Conditions." The Economic World. June 1921.

Wang, Chin Chung. "The Hankow-Szuchuan Railway Loan."
        American Journal of International Law.
        Volume 5. July 1911.

INDEX

AMERICAN BUSINESS ABROAD

Origins and Development
of the Multinational Corporation

An Arno Press Collection

Abrahams, Paul Philip. *The Foreign Expansion of American Finance and its Relationship to the Foreign Economic Policies of the United States, 1907-1921.* 1976

Adams, Frederick Upham. *Conquest of the Tropics:* The Story of the Creative Enterprises Conducted by the United Fruit Company. 1914

Arnold, Dean Alexander. *American Economic Enterprises in Korea, 1895-1939.* 1976

Bain, H. Foster and Thomas Thornton Read. *Ores and Industry in South America.* 1934

Brewster, Kingman, Jr. *Antitrust and American Business Abroad.* 1958

Callis, Helmut G. *Foreign Capital in Southeast Asia.* 1942

Crowther, Samuel. *The Romance and Rise of the American Tropics.* 1929

Davids, Jules. *American Political and Economic Penetration of Mexico, 1877-1920.* 1976

Davies, Robert Bruce. *Peacefully Working to Conquer the World:* Singer Sewing Machines in Foreign Markets, 1854-1920. 1976

de la Torre, Jose R., Jr. *Exports of Manufactured Goods from Developing Countries.* 1976

Dunn, Robert W. *American Foreign Investments.* 1926

Dunning, John H. *American Investment in British Manufacturing Industry.* 1958

Edelberg, Guillermo S. *The Procurement Practices of the Mexican Affiliates of Selected United States Automobile Firms.* 1976

Edwards, Corwin. *Economic and Political Aspects of International Cartels.* 1944

Elliott, William Yandell, Elizabeth S. May, J.W.F. Rowe, Alex Skelton, Donald H. Wallace. *International Control in the Non-Ferrous Metals.* 1937

Estimates of United States Direct Foreign Investment, 1929-1943 and 1947. 1976

Eysenbach, Mary Locke. *American Manufactured Exports, 1879-1914.* 1976

Gates, Theodore R., assisted by Fabian Linden. *Production Costs Here and Abroad.* 1958

Gordon, Wendell C. *The Expropriation of Foreign-Owned Property in Mexico.* 1941

Hufbauer, G. C. and F. M. Adler. *Overseas Manufacturing Investment and the Balance of Payments.* 1968

Lewis, Cleona, assisted by Karl T. Schlotterbeck. *America's Stake in International Investments.* 1938

McKenzie, F[red] A. *The American Invaders.* 1902

Moore, John Robert. *The Impact of Foreign Direct Investment on an Underdeveloped Economy: The Venezuelan* Case. 1976

National Planning Association. *The Creole Petroleum Corporation in Venezuela.* 1955

National Planning Association. *The Firestone Operations in Liberia*. 1956

National Planning Association. *The General Electric Company in Brazil*. 1961

National Planning Association. *Stanvac in Indonesia*. 1957

National Planning Association. *The United Fruit Company in Latin America*. 1958

Nordyke, James W. *International Finance and New York*. 1976

O'Connor, Harvey. *The Guggenheims*. 1937

Overlach, T[heodore] W. *Foreign Financial Control in China*. 1919

Pamphlets on American Business Abroad. 1976

Phelps, Clyde William. *The Foreign Expansion of American Banks*. 1927

Porter, Robert P. *Industrial Cuba*. 1899

Queen, George Sherman. *The United States and the Material Advance in Russia, 1881-1906*. 1976

Rippy, J. Fred. *The Capitalists and Colombia*. 1931

Southard, Frank A., Jr. *American Industry in Europe*. 1931

Staley, Eugene. *Raw Materials in Peace and War*. 1937

Statistics on American Business Abroad, 1950-1975. 1976

Stern, Siegfried. *The United States in International Banking*. 1952

U.S. Congress. House of Representatives. Committee on Foreign Affairs. *The Overseas Private Investment Corporation*. 1973

U.S. Congress. Senate. Special Committee Investigating Petroleum Resources. *American Petroleum Interests in Foreign Countries*. 1946

U.S. Dept. of Commerce. Office of Business Economics. *U.S. Business Investments in Foreign Countries*. 1960

U.S. Dept. of Commerce. Office of Business Economics. *U.S. Investments in the Latin American Economy*. [1957]

U.S. Dept. of Commerce and Labor. *Report of the Commissioner of Corporations on the Petroleum Industry:* Part III, Foreign Trade. 1909

U.S. Federal Trade Commission. *The International Petroleum Cartel*. 1952

Vanderlip, Frank A. *The American "Commercial Invasion" of Europe*. 1902

Winkler, Max. *Foreign Bonds, an Autopsy:* A Study of Defaults and Repudiations of Government Obligations. 1933

Yeoman, Wayne A. *Selection of Production Processes for the Manufacturing Subsidiaries of U.S.-Based Multinational Corporations*. 1976

Yudin, Elinor Barry. *Human Capital Migration, Direct Investment and the Transfer of Technology:* An Examination of Americans Privately Employed Overseas. 1976